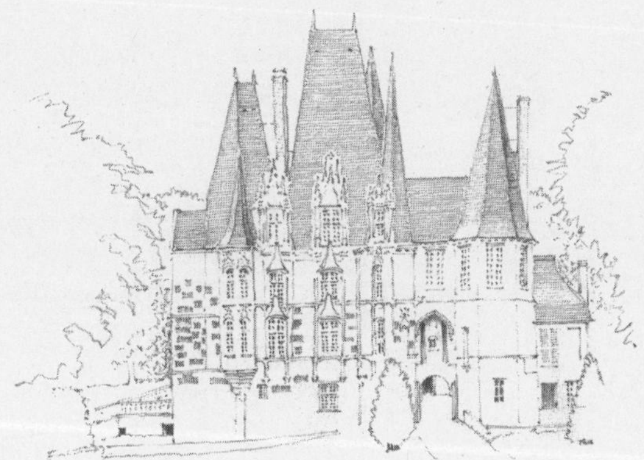

TRAVELS with JAN, pen & 2B

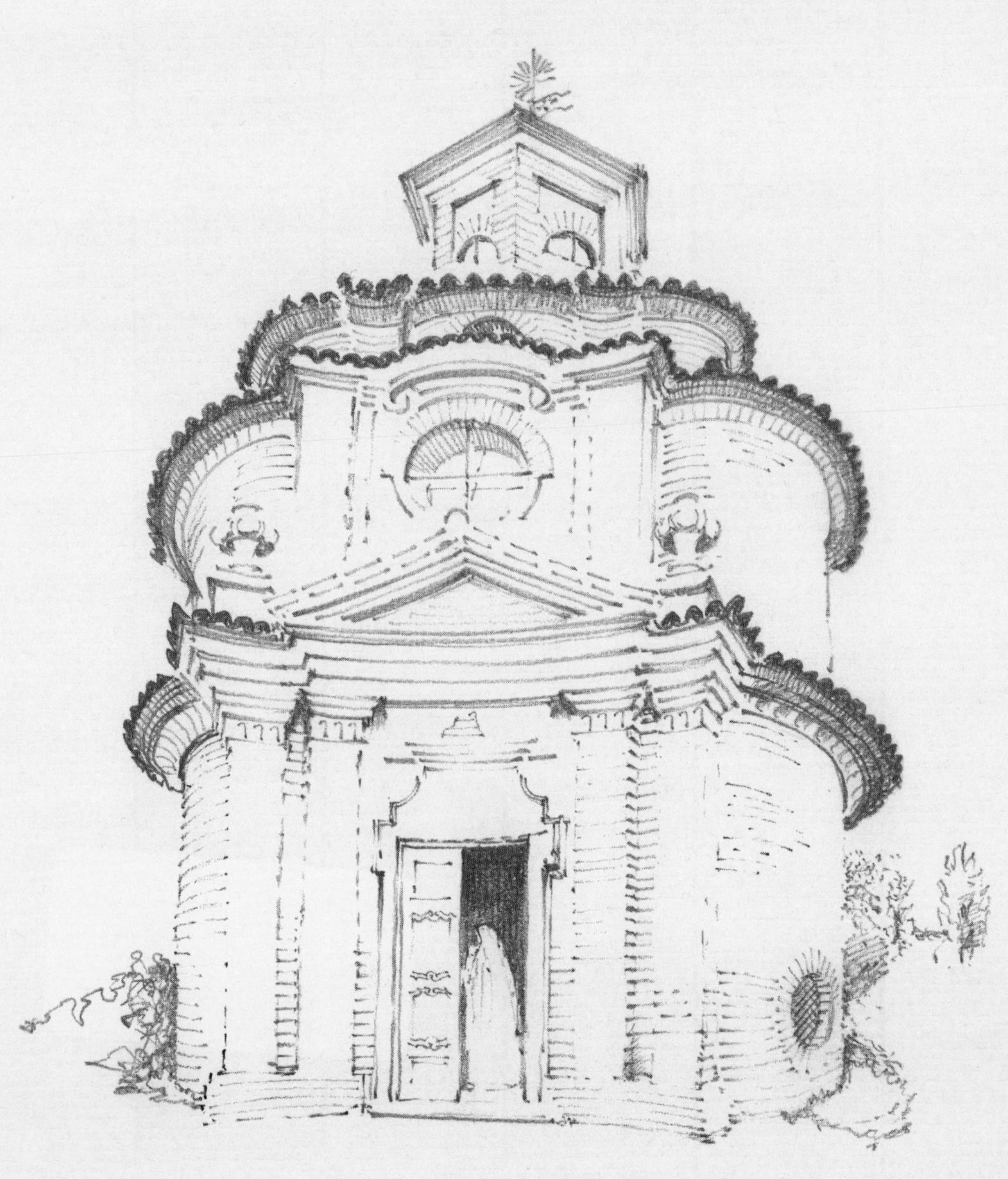

CORTERANZO Funerary Chapel (Vittone)

TRAVELS

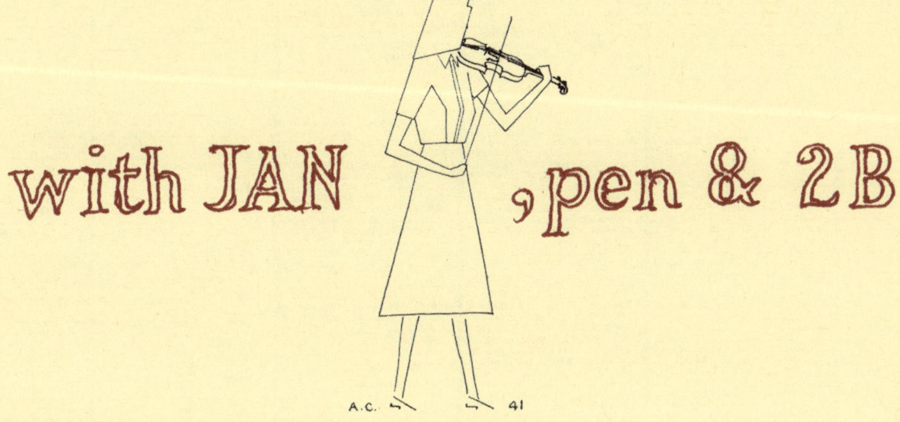

with JAN, pen & 2B

Antony
Cleminson

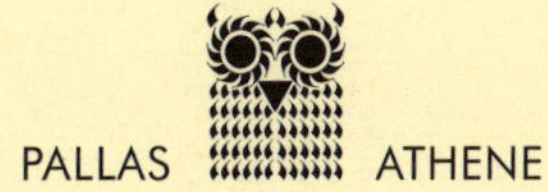

PALLAS ATHENE

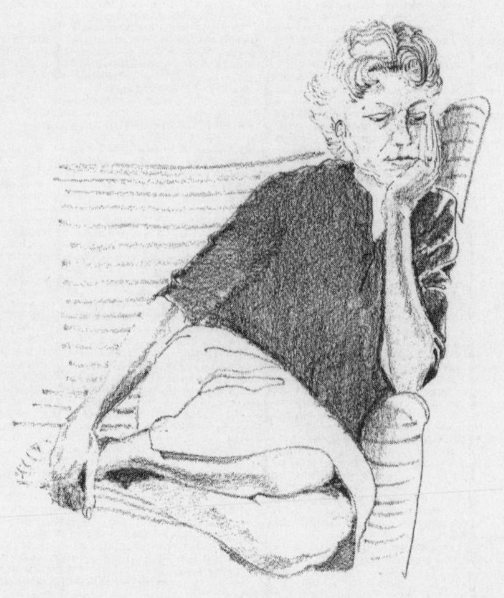

I should like to dedicate this sketchbook
to JAN, the ideal Travelling Companion in
every sense, on our 64th Anniversary.

Think of the 120 x 2 hours of hanging about
while I drew these – plus the same again for
those not included – plenty of books read.

My grateful thanks to Alexander Fyjis Walker
who brought the whole project to fruition
with his skill, knowledge and dedication.

Also to Colin Amery for introducing us.

Antony Clemenson 2 Jan 09

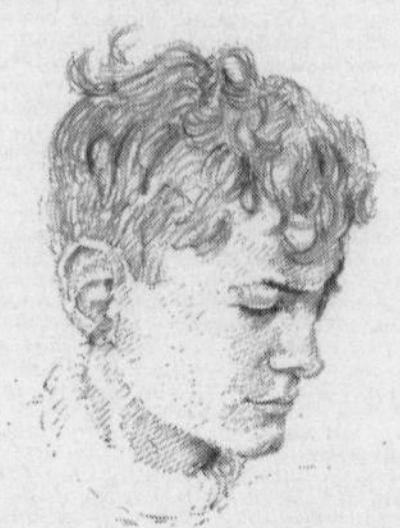

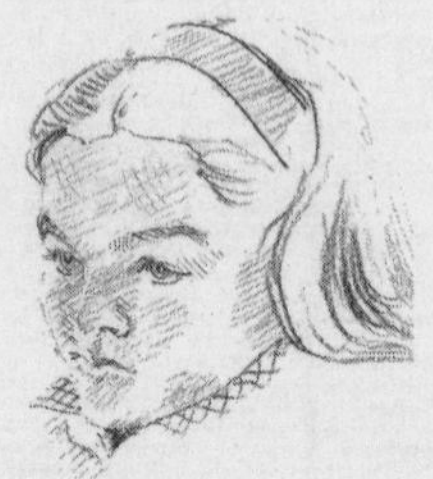

FOREWORD

Two strong memories remain. The sounds of a quartet drifting down from open windows on a summer evening in a Georgian London street – the notes reverberating and the music ending in gales of laughter. The other indelible memory – my first meeting with tall, thin Antony in the elegant, almost Spartan, rooms of No. 27 Upper Montagu Street when I became his tenant and having long discussions about eighteenth century architectural attributions. Architecture and music filled that house.

It was a brave move when Antony decided to leave his business career and enrol as a student at the Architectural Association in 1974. It was a decision that enabled him to unite his technical enthusiasms with his powers of trained observation. Antony loves buildings and the consistent integrity of his drawings reveals a lifetime of steady looking and recording. You can sense from this sketchbook his love, not just of travelling but also of architectural discovery shared by Jan's objective and almost detached view of the world.

They have travelled together from Russia to the Yemen and through most of Europe in between and it is all here recorded in the tranquillity of a long and settled marriage and a beautifully ordered life. There is a discipline here that respects the edifices and architectural language of the past and wants to understand both the technical and creative processes that underline architectural achievement. It is interesting that every single drawing in this book is an exterior view leaving us to exercise our imagination about the interior worlds. I sense Antony is most at home in Italy and France with a hint of a bias towards the resolved simplicity of the Romanesque style. The churches of the Pyrenees both East and West, all one hundred and forty four of them are recorded here. Antony's enthusiastic discovery of the fortified churches of the Thiérache region of France – some fifty of them – reveals his knowledgeable patience as the recording angel of Europe's deep and wonderful architectural inheritance. I will always be glad that I know this unchanging couple reading and drawing in the heart of London – perhaps travelling a bit less now – and Antony's sketchbook will always remind us how marvellous architecture and drawing can be.

Colin Amery

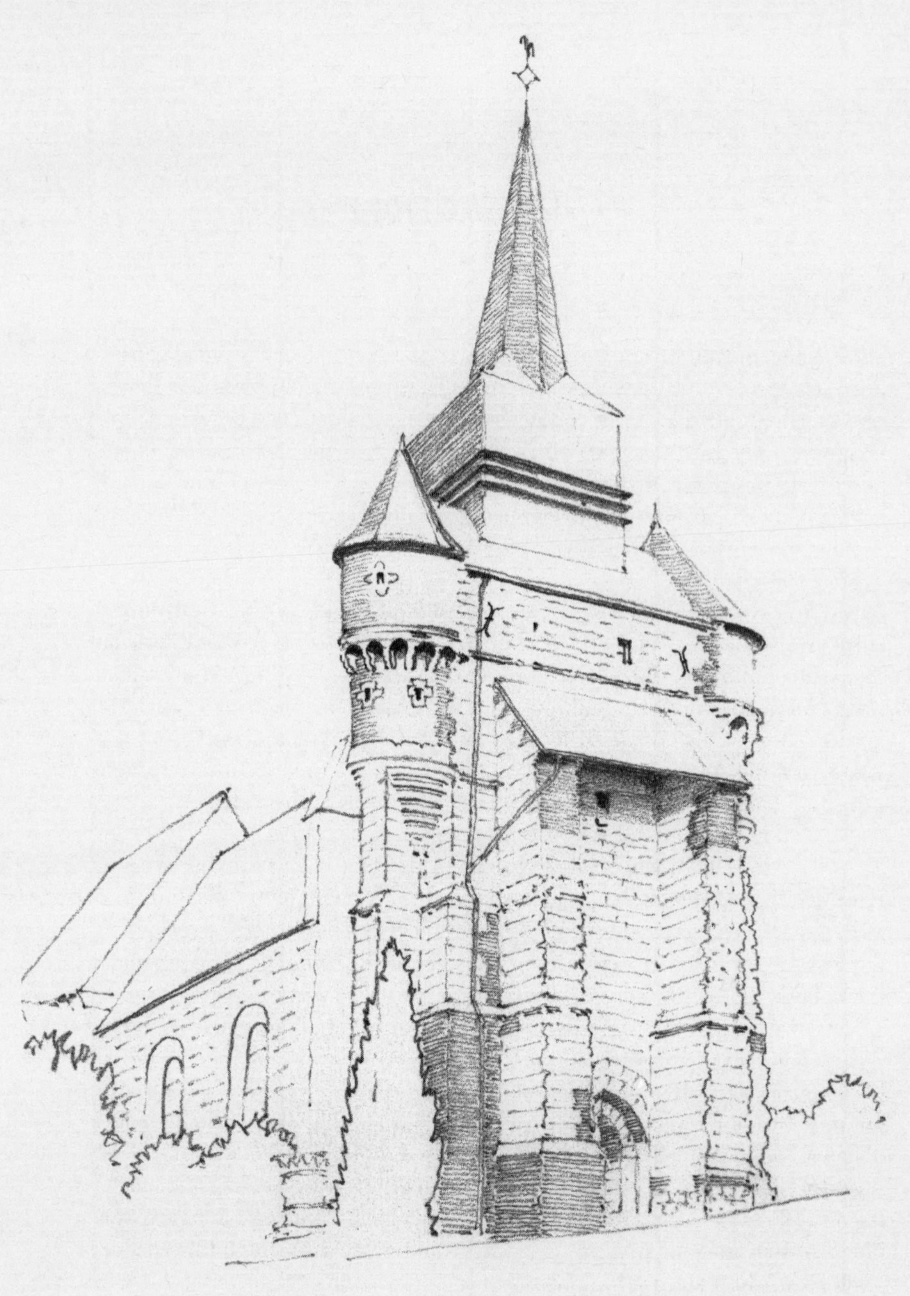

MACQUIGNY 04

For Antony

Algasmy, Zafra, Tardebigge. Le Château d'O: such
Names alone can ravish us. Yet eyes demand their due:
To ink the heft of stone, the air of arch, huddle
Of houses on a hill, with such assured delight:
Narthex and bartizan, roughness of roof tiles,
Yemeni minarets, La Granja's finials –
St John's, Smith Square in a cascade of birds or leaves –

This is your art, intensity of patience
Rare as skill, a way of inking lines
As resonant as tuned, plucked strings:
Viola's charm, and substance. All those afternoons or
Evenings, drawing, in the company of lifelong
Love: the one who, lost in a book, that most perfect captivity,
Stays close to you as pen to paper.

Which of them would I elect to haunt
If, by some fiction of desire, lodging could be had in
Tower or parador of your devising? Boldo Canal,
Hadrian's Villa, each Romanesque church of the West Pyrenees?

Just a window's depth, a shaded corbel: room enough.
A glimpse of Petra through rock's jagged shutters:
No truer architecture of the heart.

Janice Kulyk Keefer

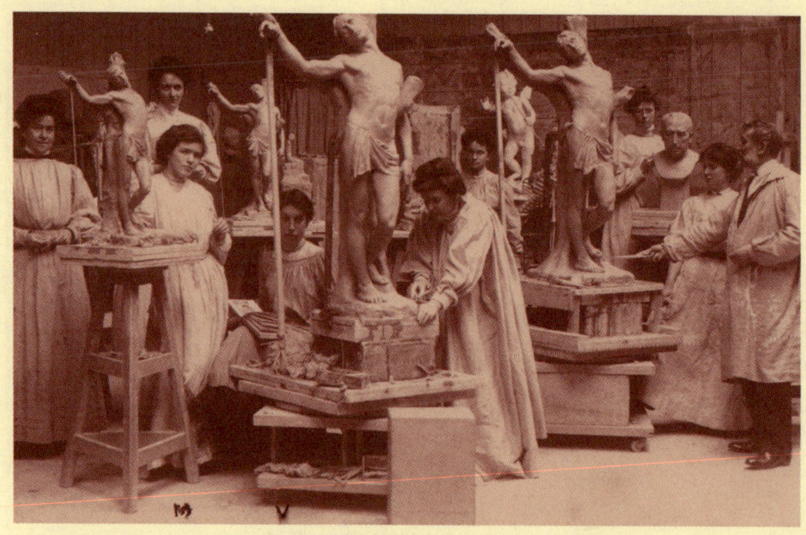

PROLOGUE

Brought up in a family where 'two minute drawings' were our regular family entertainment – we took turns to choose a subject – my mother and my older brothers were far better at it.

My mother (M in the photograph), from Canada, was a sculpture student at the Royal College of Art before the First World War, and exhibited at the Royal Academy as a student in 1908 and 1910.

My elder brother Howard was a natural artist and distinguished himself as a student at the Architectural Association in the late thirties before he died in 1939, midway through his studies.

At fifteen Howard took me, aged twelve, to France to stay with our sculptress aunt (V in the photograph), who lived in La Bergerie, Houx par Maintenon (drawing opposite by Howard).

Jackie Fisher as First Lord of the Admiralty – the great moderniser – thought that every 'deck' officer in a recently mechanised navy ought to be aware of the panic he was causing down below if he suddenly ordered 'full speed astern'. So instead of learning Latin at Dartmouth, where I went in 1935, one did what was the equivalent of an H. N. C. Engineering course. This involved the usual technical disciplines – carpentry, pattern-making, smithy, foundry and a couple of hours a week in the Drawing Office making engineering drawings. This I much enjoyed whereas my contemporaries were less enthusiastic, and I became able in exams to make passable images of the drawings shown to us in lectures so that I came top in both intermediate and final engineering order of my term. But I had no wish to be stuck below at sea.

As Midshipmen (1939-40) we were obliged to keep a journal with sketches of technical arrangements – for mine-sweeping for example – and this I enjoyed more than most of my contemporaries.

When I left the Navy in 1948 and joined a manufacturing firm I was astonished to find that I seemed alone in understanding engineering drawings.

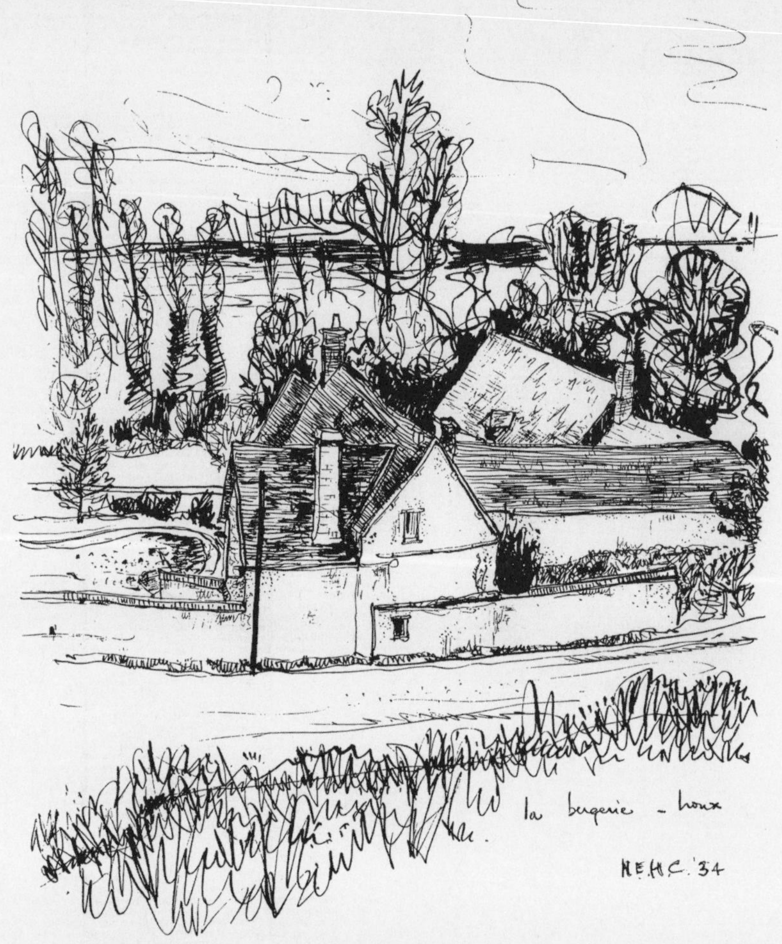

Everything was made from templates. I later became the (Technical) Sales Director for twenty years which involved little sales but technical advice to car designers (mostly sculptors by training) in solid geometry and optical problems. This was a fascinating world, particularly among the specialist designers in Turin, many of whom worked as consultants to British car manufacturers and the world over.

But clients, short of the occasional component, would ring endlessly for help, and the day became oppressive at times. As a perfect antidote, my wife and daughter took me to the London Polytechnic and encouraged me to enlist at the evening life class. The first night the life class was full, so I was sent to the sculpture class where there were vacancies.

After my first try the teacher asked me perceptively: 'Is this your first attempt?' 'Yes,' I said. 'How do you go about it?' and she took my pad and drew a block of stone and then pared it down until the figure emerged. The next week, back in the life drawing class, I asked the teacher there how *he* went about it, and he demonstrated a sort of triangulation survey method that he used. 'Chacun à son goût.'

None of my life drawings is included, but they are essential training.

Holidays on the continent then became an ever more frequent delight, and this volume starts from there.

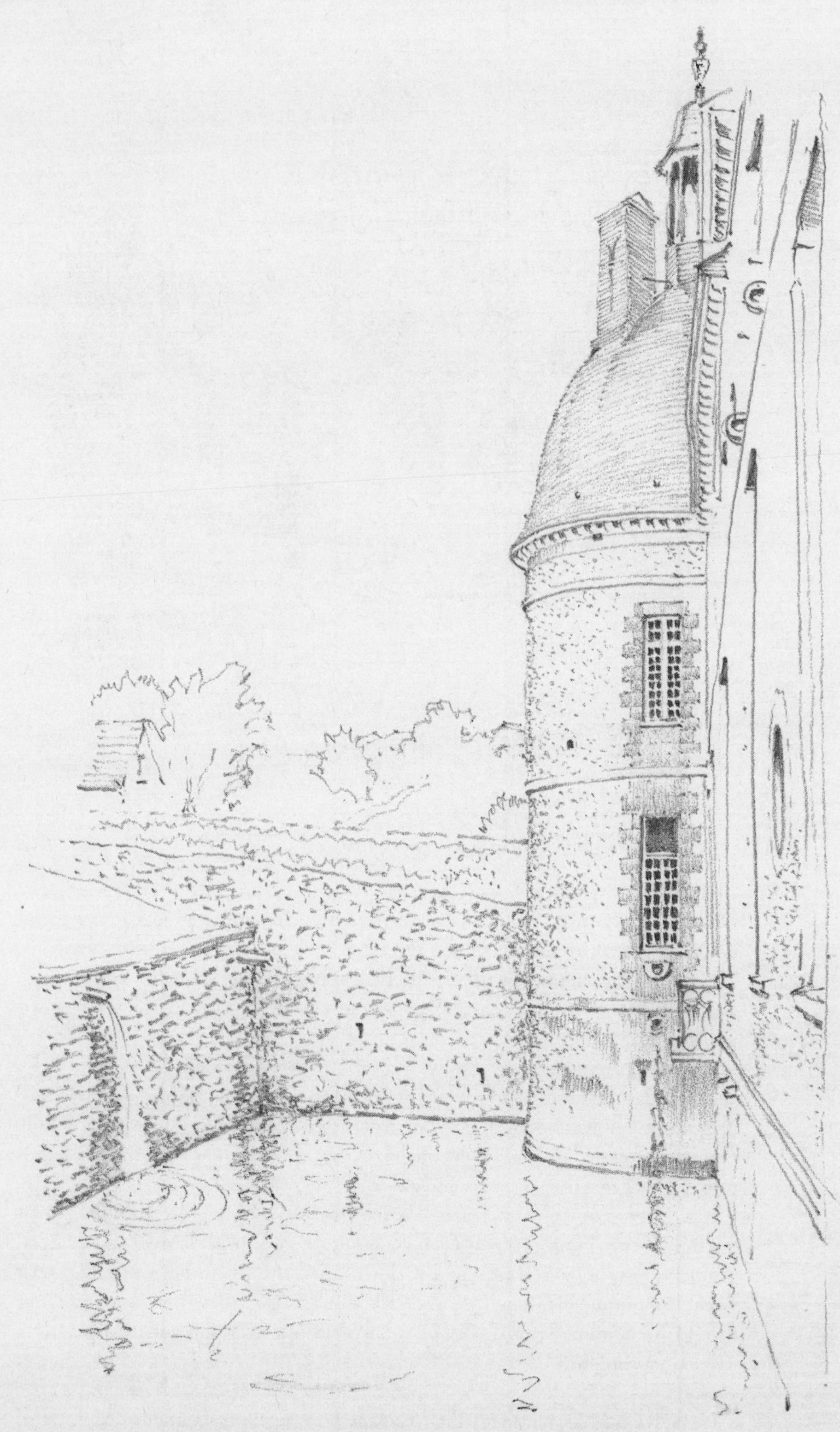

CHATEAU D'ETOGES A.C.04

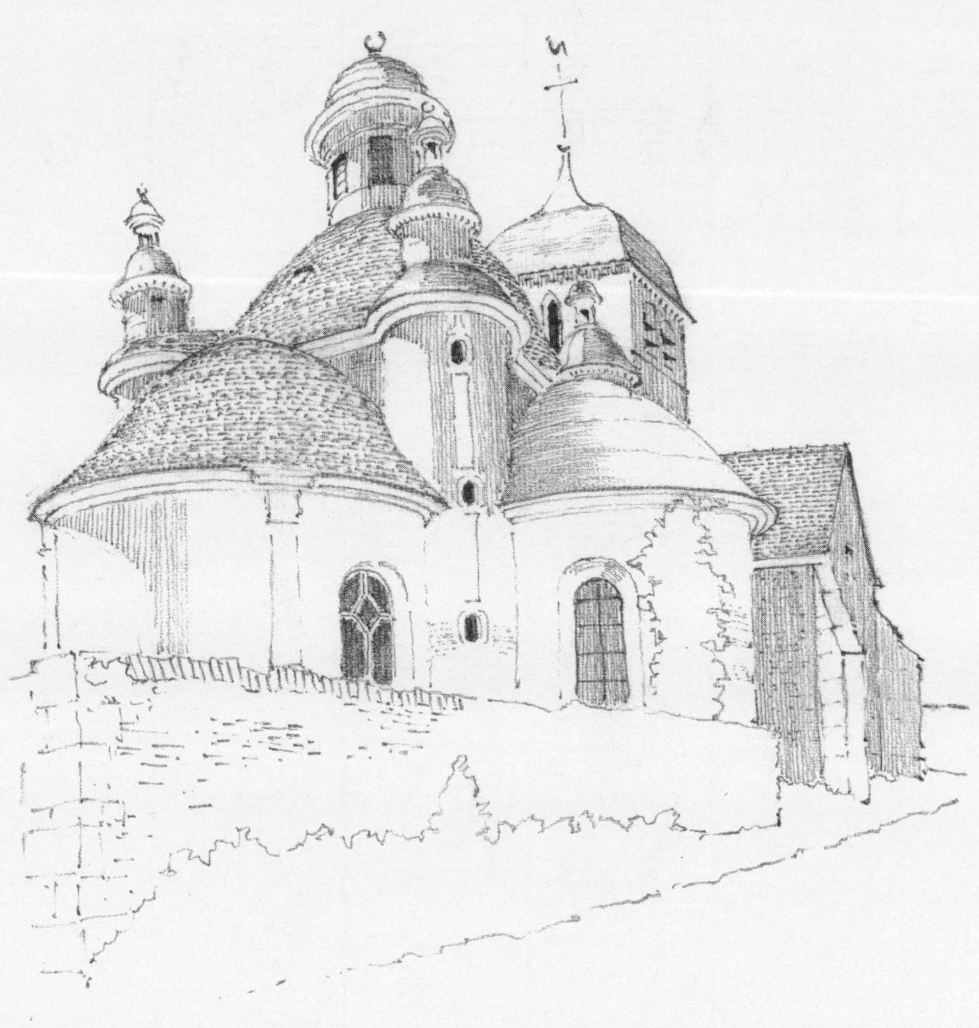

PARGUES

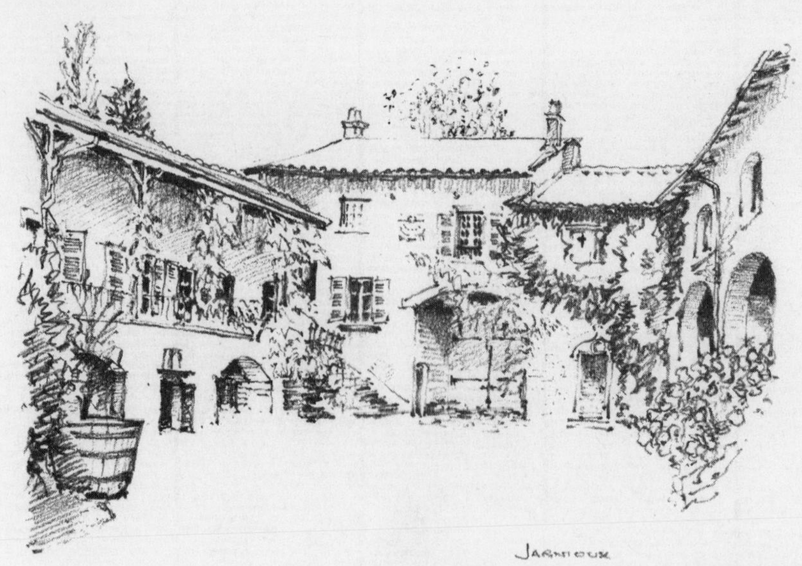

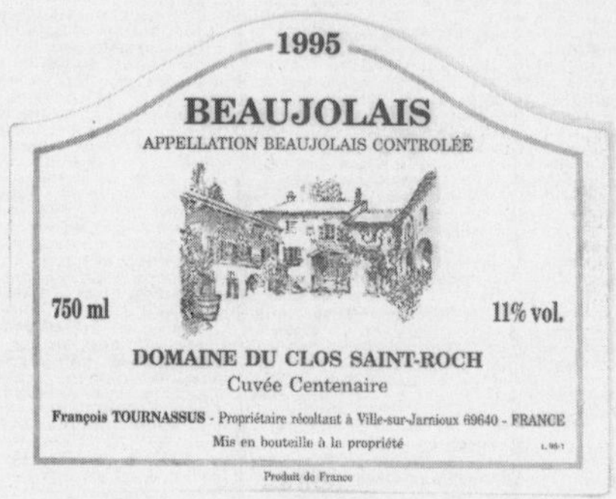
1995
BEAUJOLAIS
APPELLATION BEAUJOLAIS CONTROLÉE
750 ml
11% vol.
DOMAINE DU CLOS SAINT-ROCH
Cuvée Centenaire
François TOURNASSUS - Propriétaire récoltant à Ville-sur-Jarnioux 69640 - FRANCE
Mis en bouteille à la propriété
Produit de France

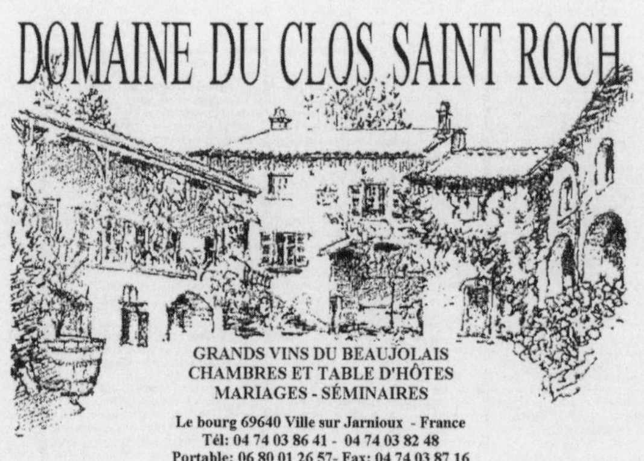
DOMAINE DU CLOS SAINT ROCH
GRANDS VINS DU BEAUJOLAIS
CHAMBRES ET TABLE D'HÔTES
MARIAGES - SÉMINAIRES
Le bourg 69640 Ville sur Jarnioux - France
Tél: 04 74 03 86 41 - 04 74 03 82 48
Portable: 06 80 01 26 57- Fax: 04 74 03 87 16

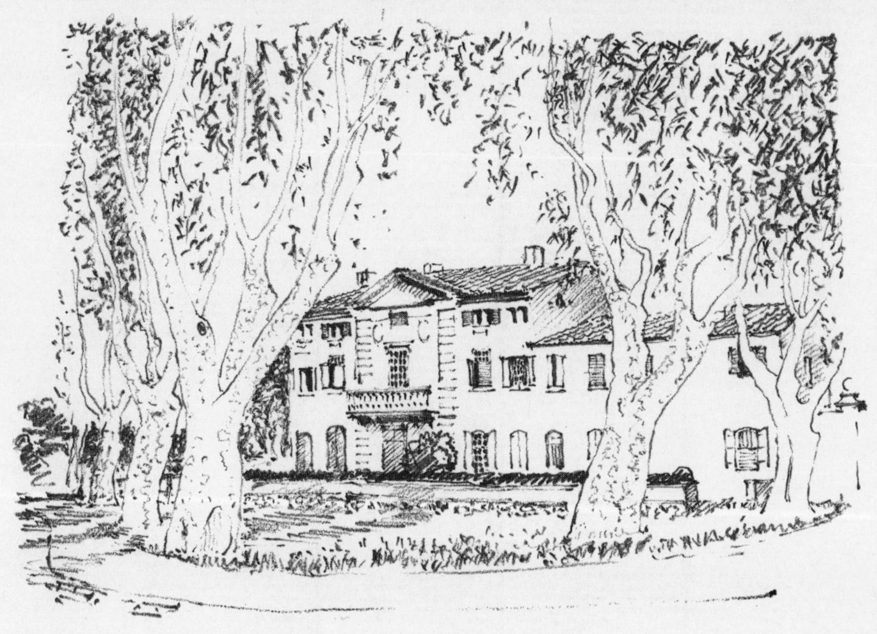

CHATEAU DE ROUSSAN FRONT

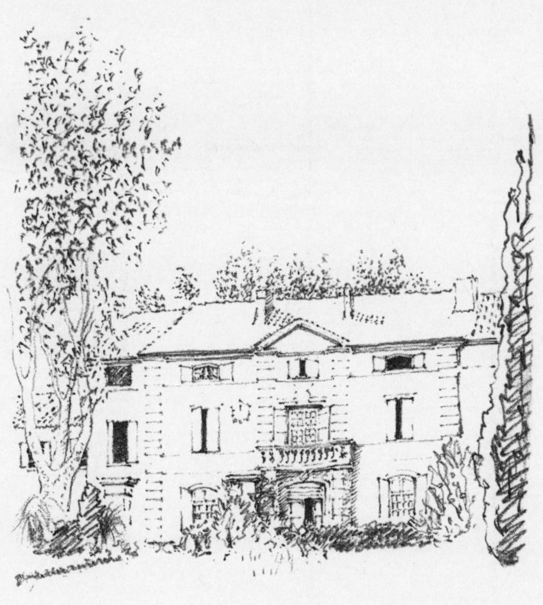

BACK A.C.72

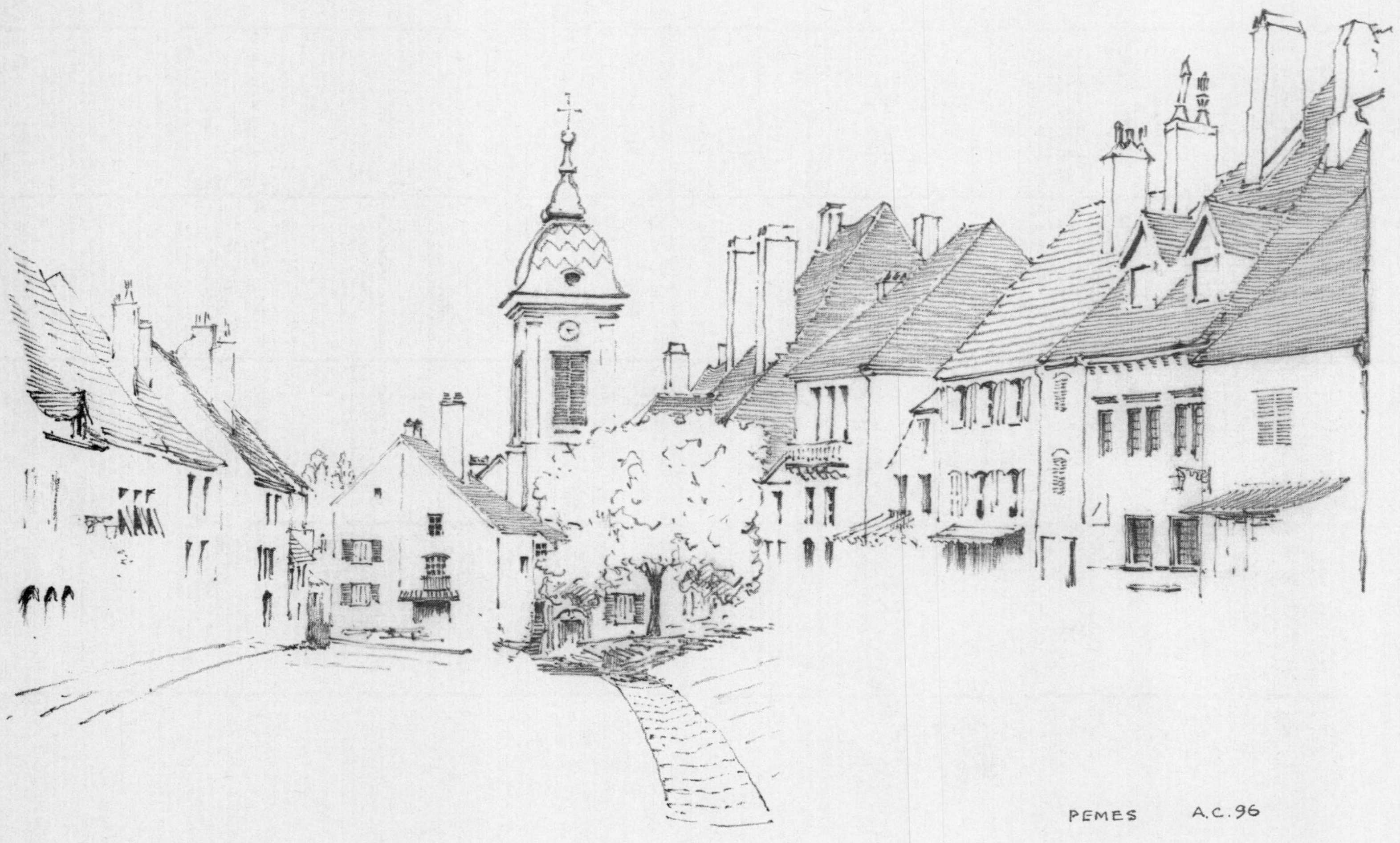
PEMES A.C.96

MANOIR DE L'ANGENARDIERE, Le PERCHE

29.9.02

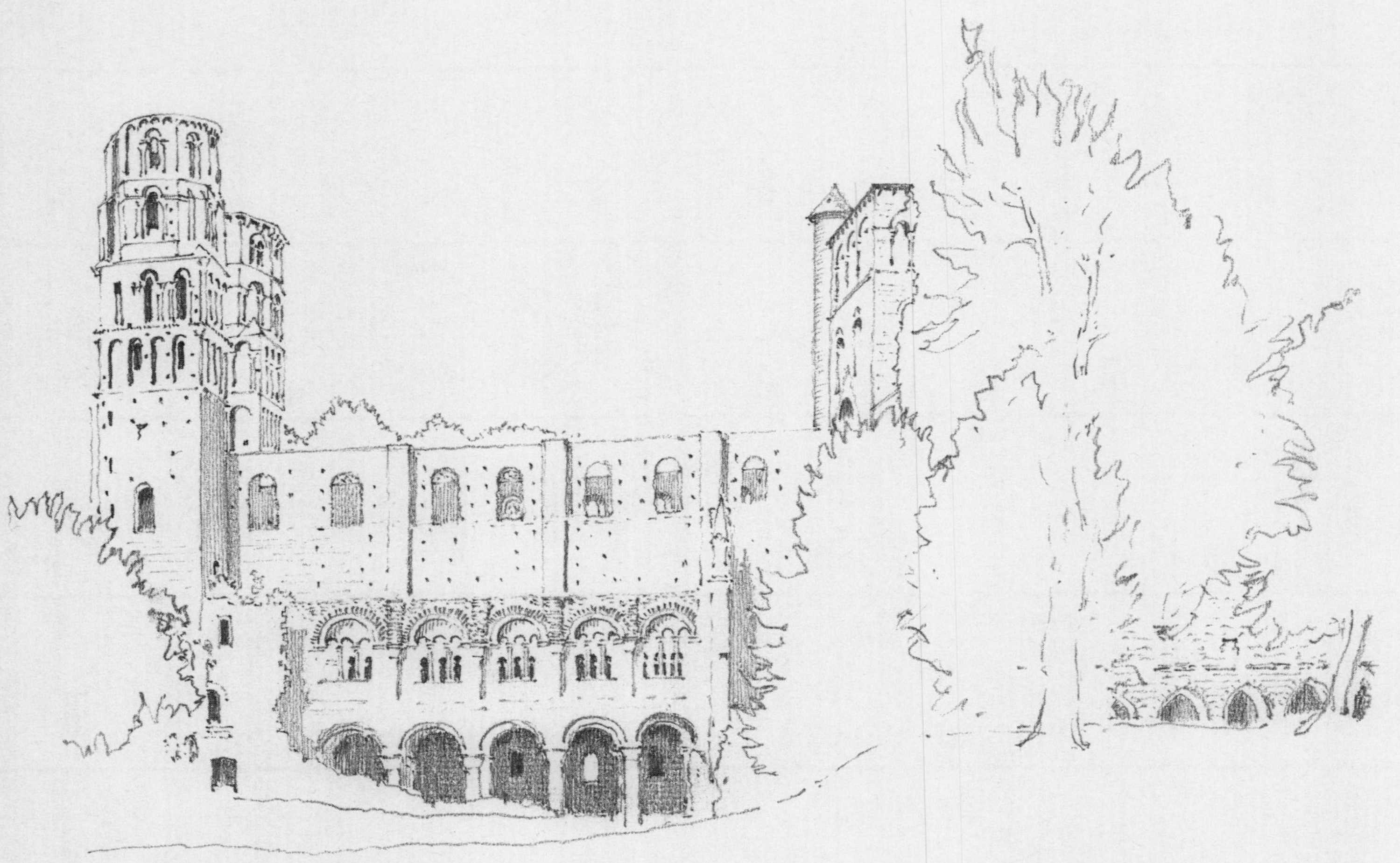

JUMIÈGES 9/02

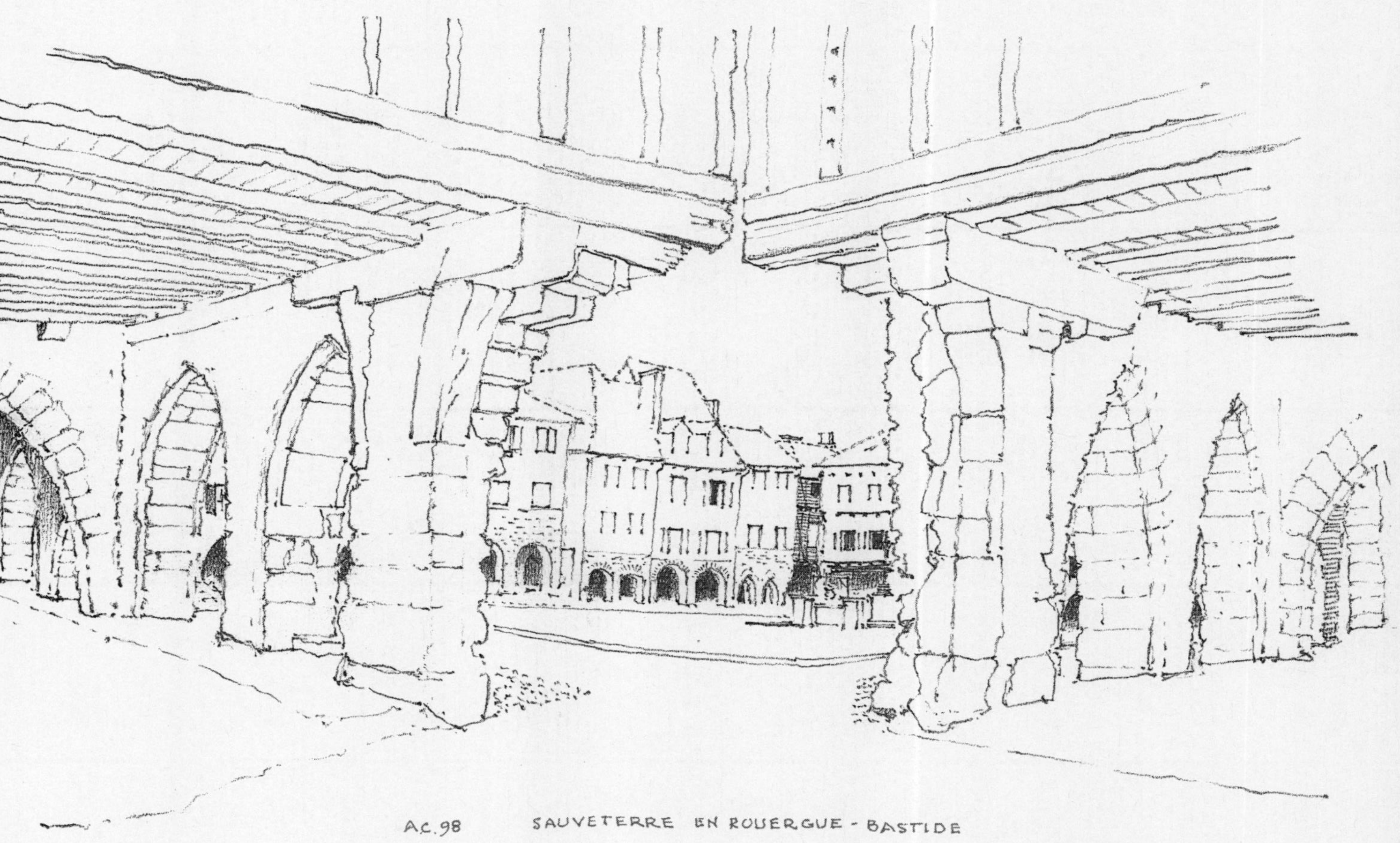

A.C. 98 SAUVETERRE EN ROUERGUE - BASTIDE

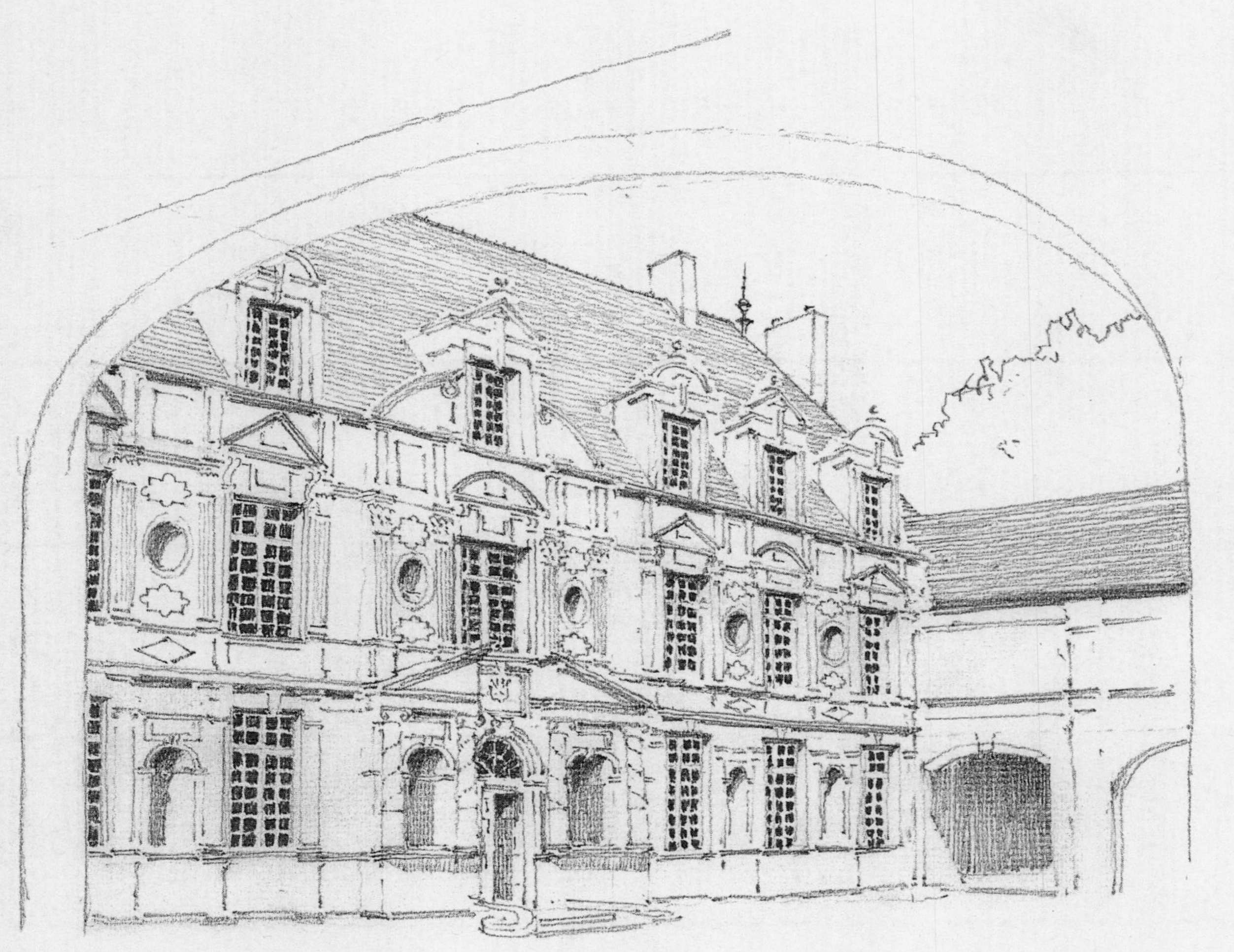

BUSSY RABUTIN

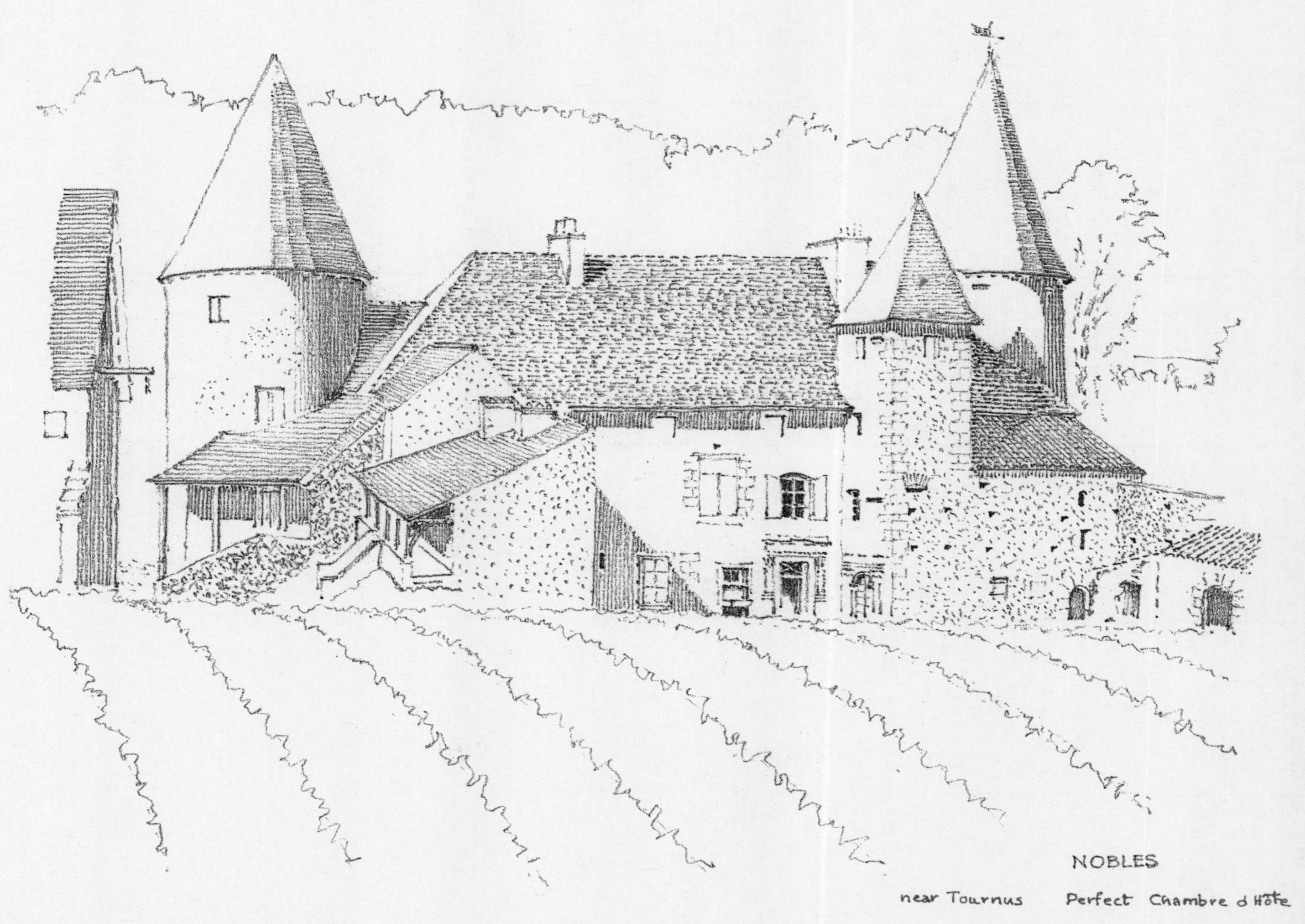

NOBLES

near Tournus   Perfect Chambre d'Hôte

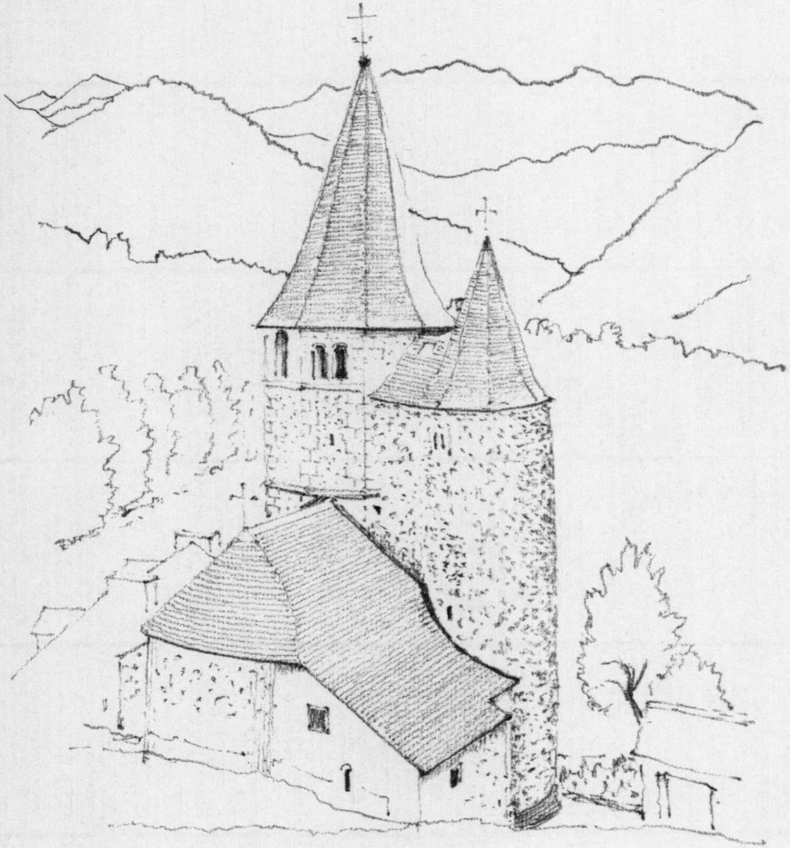

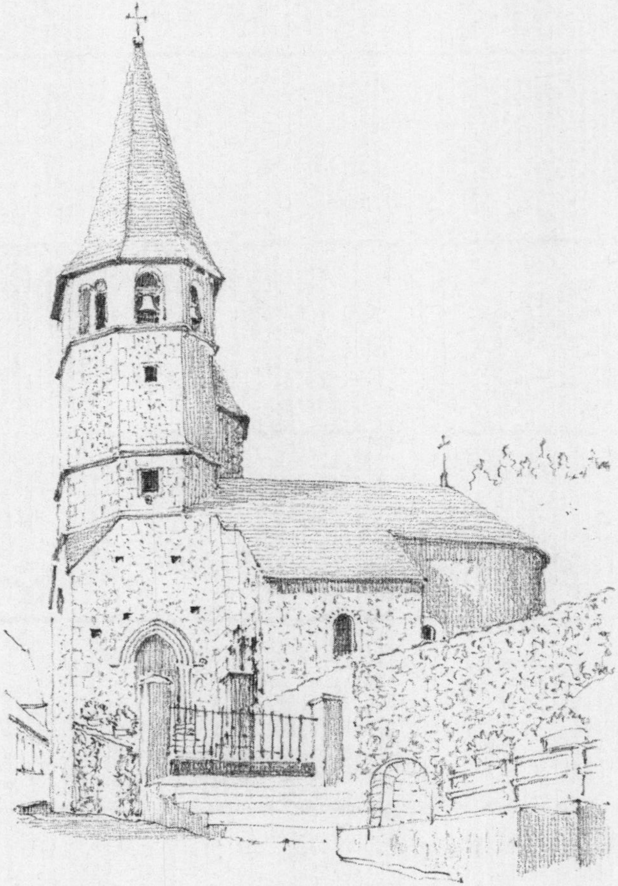

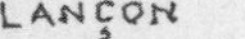
LANÇON

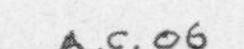
A.C. 06

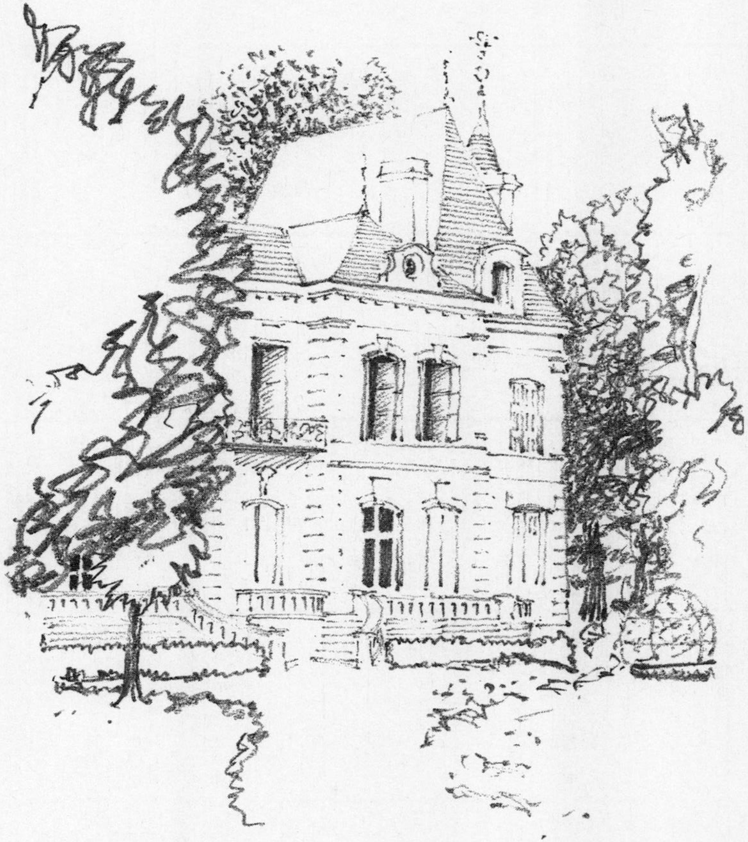

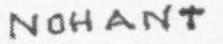

NOHANT

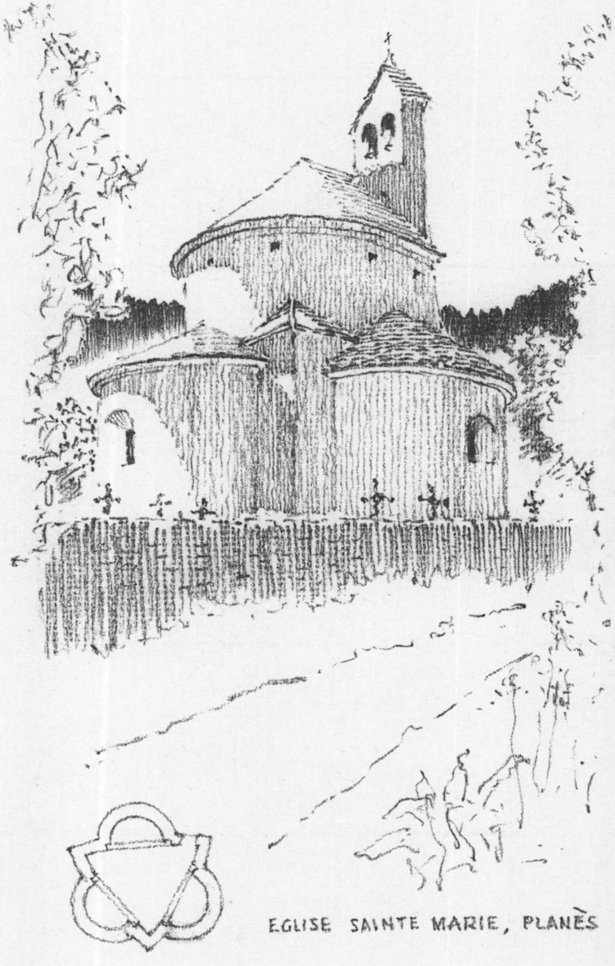

EGLISE SAINTE MARIE, PLANÈS

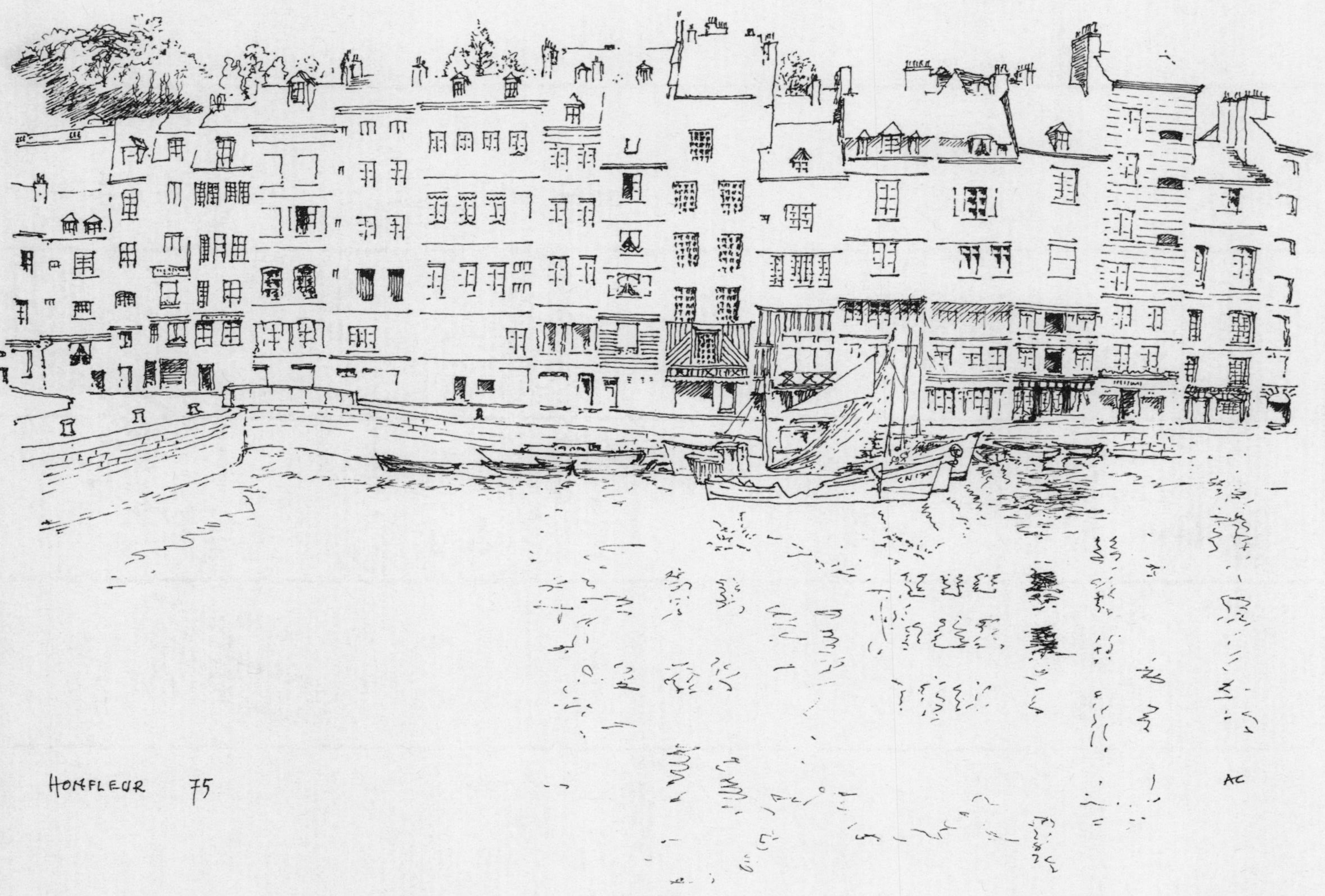
HONFLEUR 75
AC

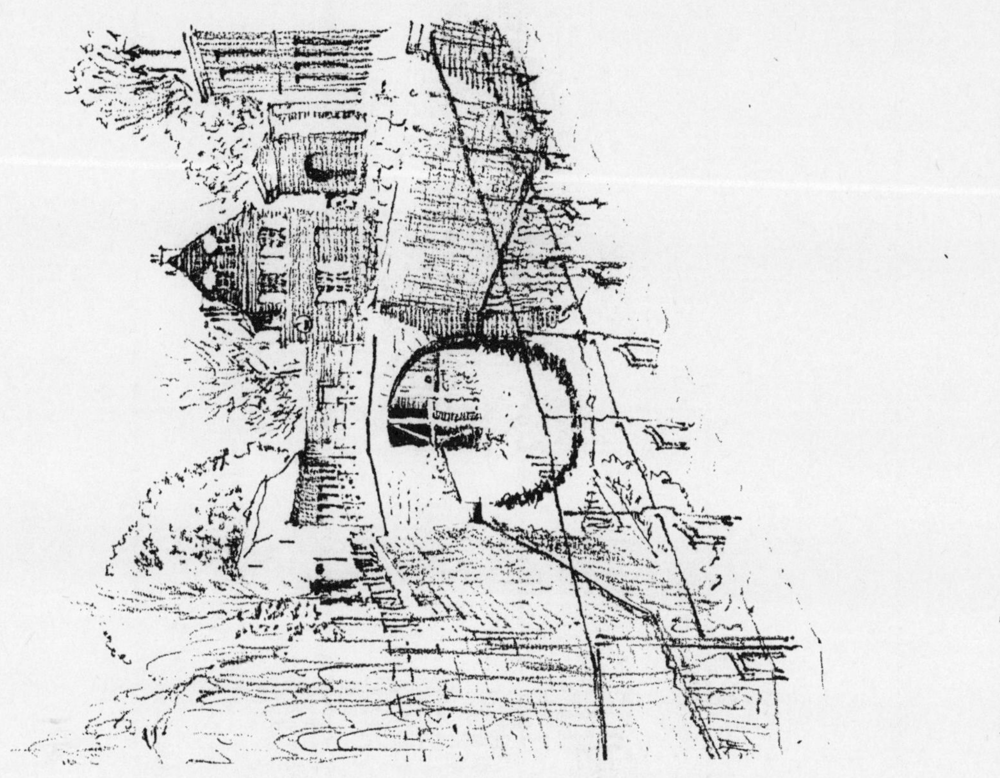

ABATTOIR AC 97 BERGUES

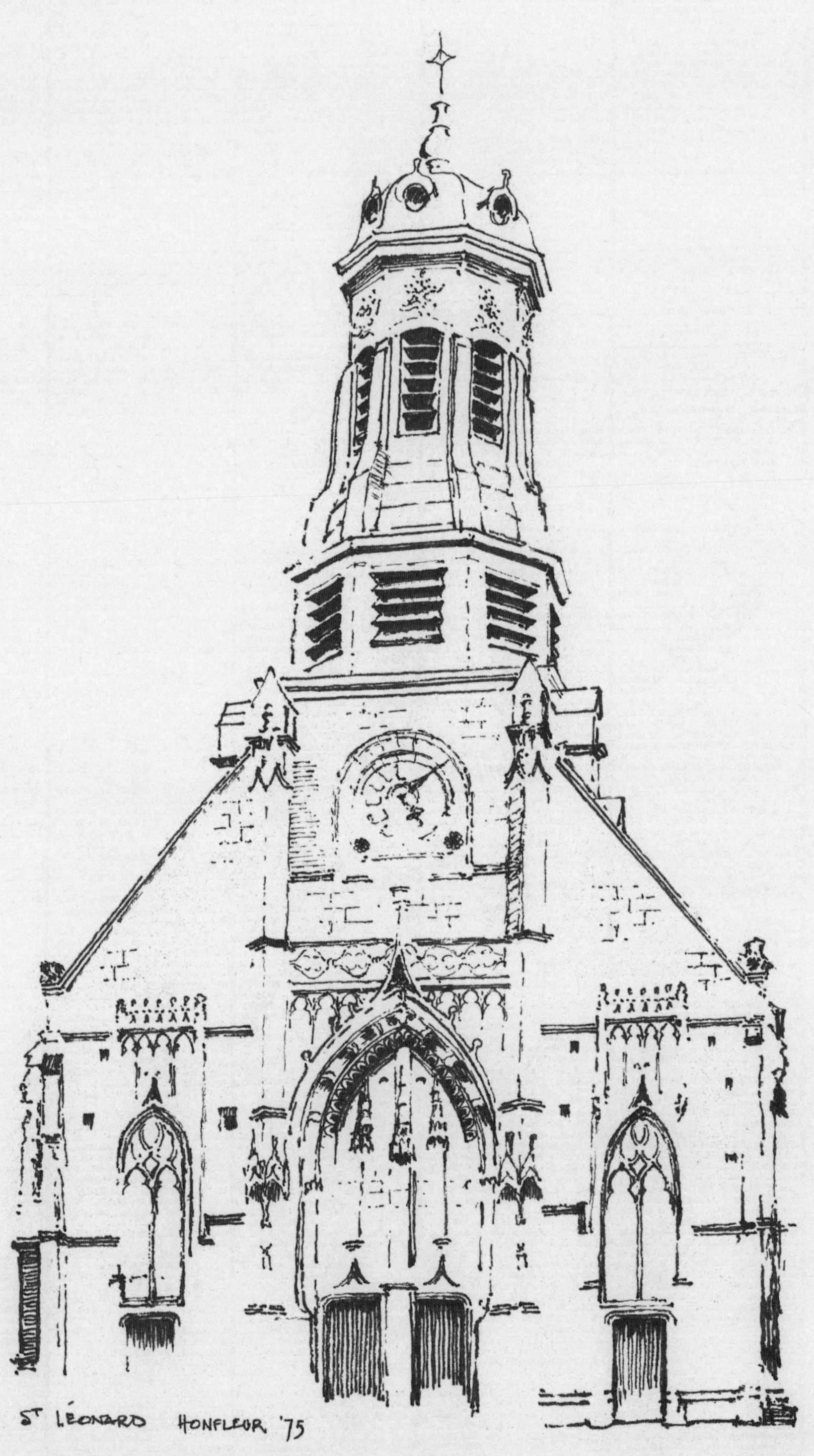
St LÉONARD HONFLEUR '75

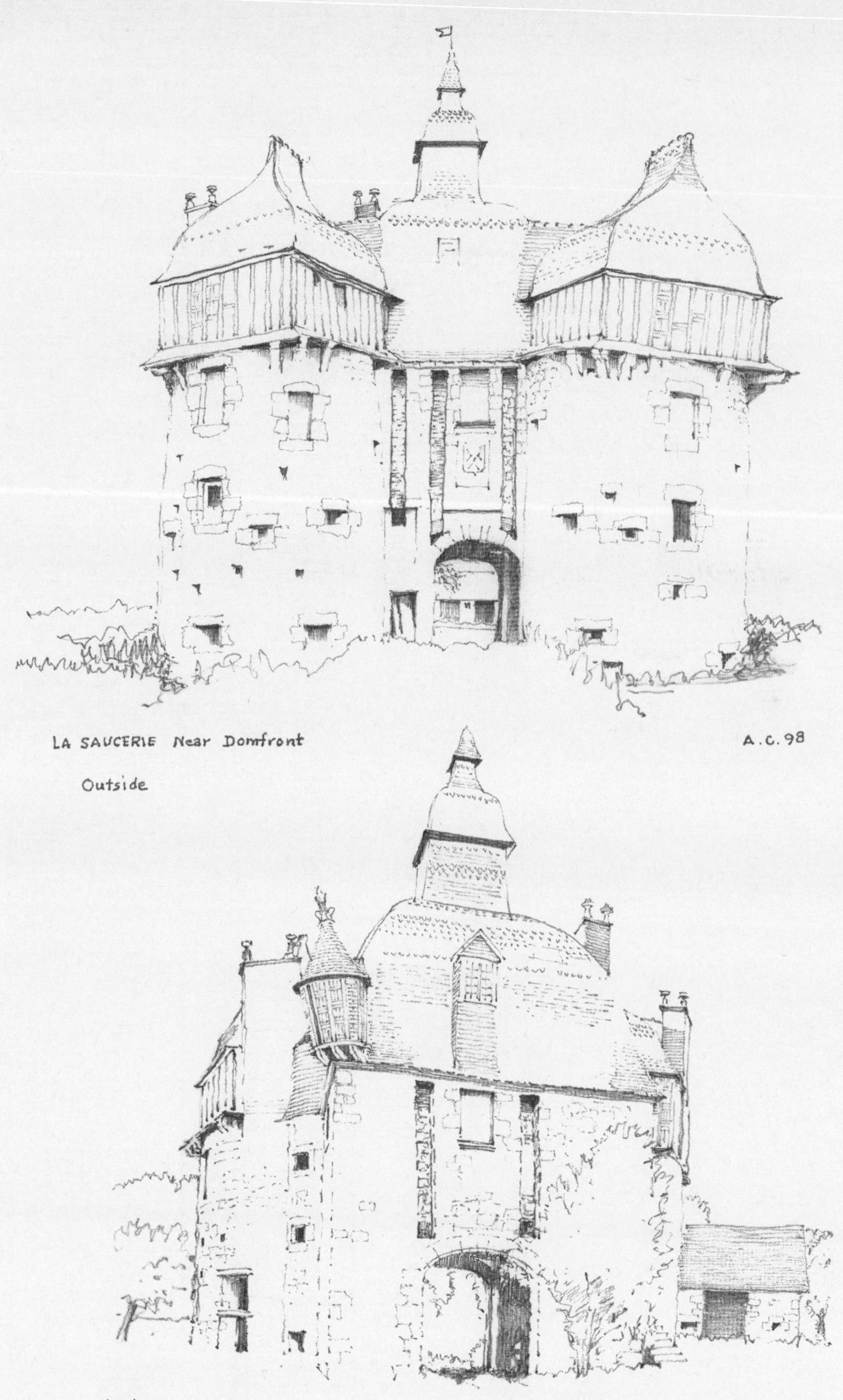

LA SAUCERIE Near Domfront

Outside

Inside

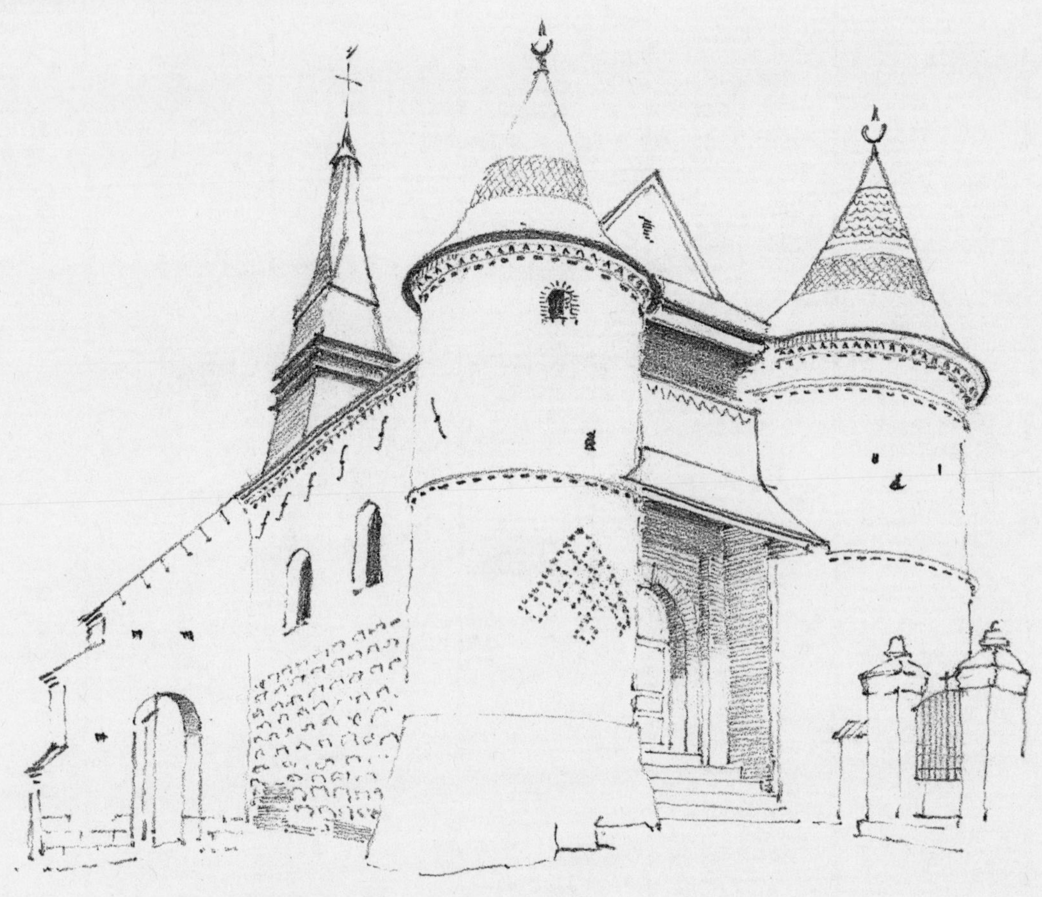

THIERACHE

The Thiérache is an area of France that is little known even by the French. It lies between Reims and the Ardennes region and was constantly overrun by various armies – the Spanish from the Netherlands, the French re-occupying them etc: To cope with these persistent invasions in the 15 th + 16 th centuries, the fifty-odd villages all fortified their churches for refuge and self defence.

All sited in a 20 mile square, they were close enough to allow visual alarm signals from church tower to church tower allowing the inhabitants to take refuge in their village church – the animals in the nave, the inhabitants in the enlarged towers with fireplaces to cook by and to sleep in the roof spaces over the nave.

They were also equipped with gun ports, arrow slits and other defensive paraphernalia.

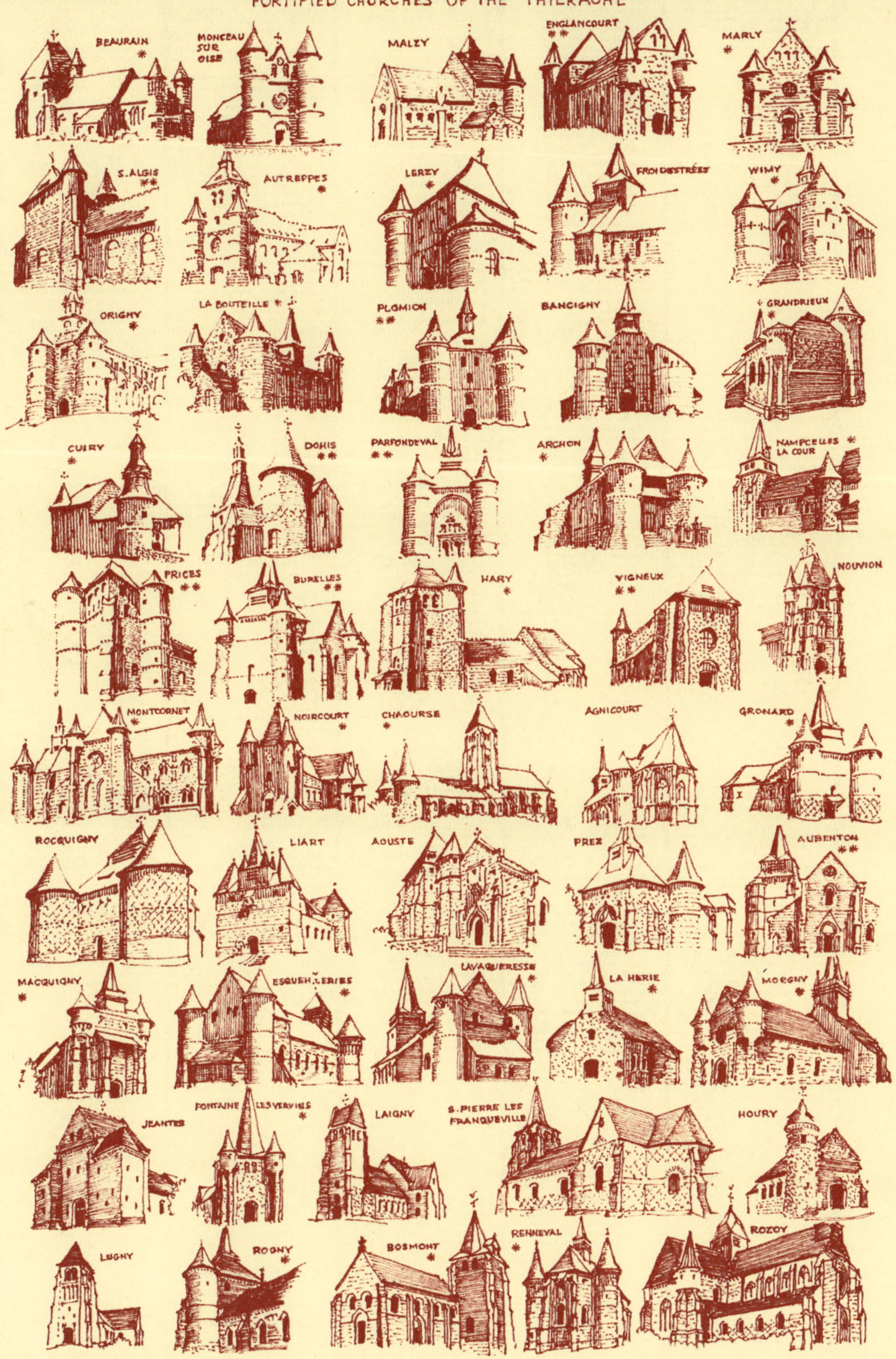
FORTIFIED CHURCHES OF THE THIÉRACHE
BEAURAIN
MONCEAU SUR OISE
MALZY
ENGLANCOURT
MARLY
S. ALGIS
AUTREPPES
LERZY
FROIDESTRÉES
WIMY
ORIGNY
LA BOUTEILLE
PLOMION
BANCIGNY
GRANDRIEUX
CUIRY
DOHIS
PARFONDEVAL
ARCHON
NAMPCELLES LA COUR
PRICES
BURELLES
HARY
VIGNEUX
NOUVION
MONTCORNET
NOIRCOURT
CHAOURSE
AGNICOURT
GRONARD
ROCQUIGNY
LIART
AOUSTE
PREZ
AUBENTON
MACQUIGNY
ESQUEHERIES
LAVAQUERESSE
LA HERIE
MORGNY
JEANTES
FONTAINE LES VERVINS
LAIGNY
S. PIERRE LES FRANQUEVILLE
HOURY
LUGNY
ROGNY
BOSMONT
RENNEVAL
ROZOY

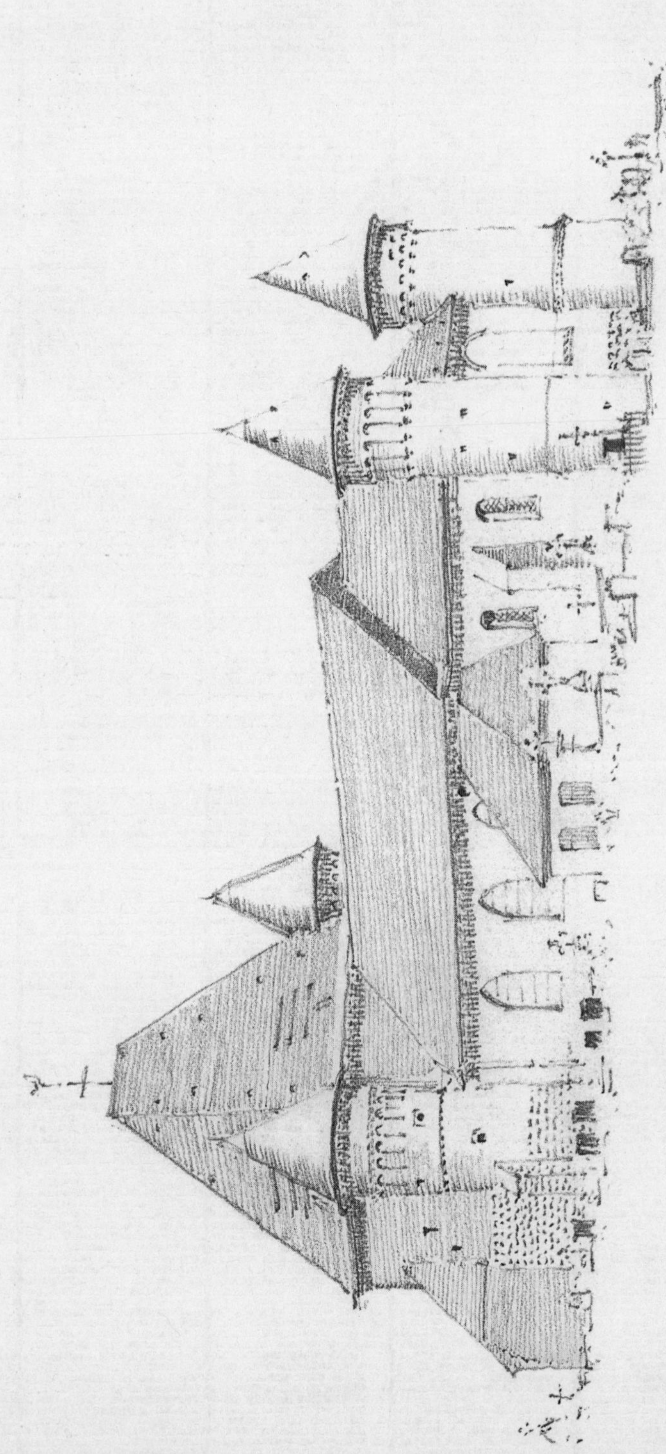

BEAURAIN Ac 04

PLOMION Le HUTEAU Best Thiérache Restaurant. Book ahead. 04

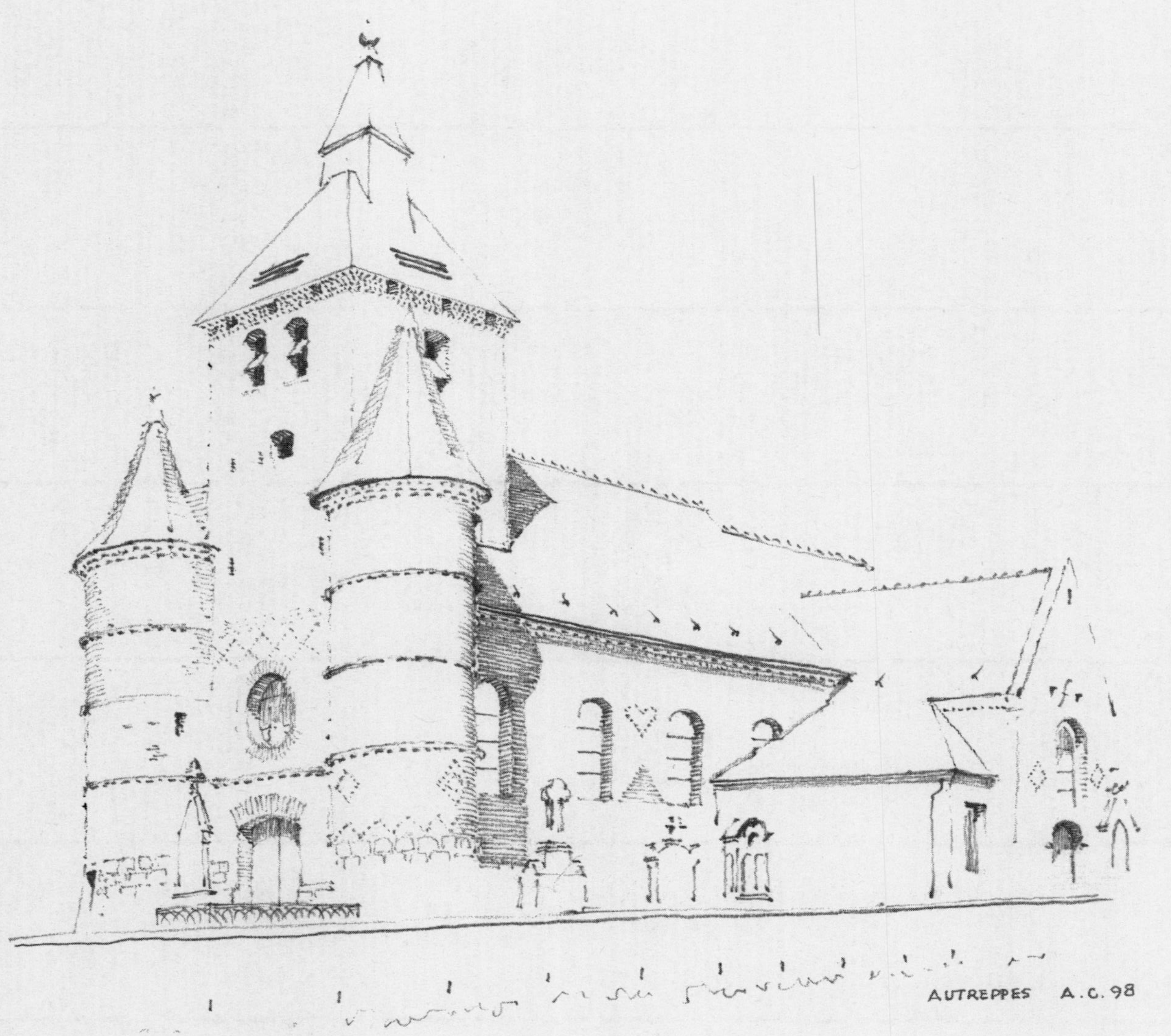
AUTREPPES A.C. 98

COUR DES PRES, RUMIGNY. Ideal Chambre d'Hôte for the Thiérache. A.C. 04

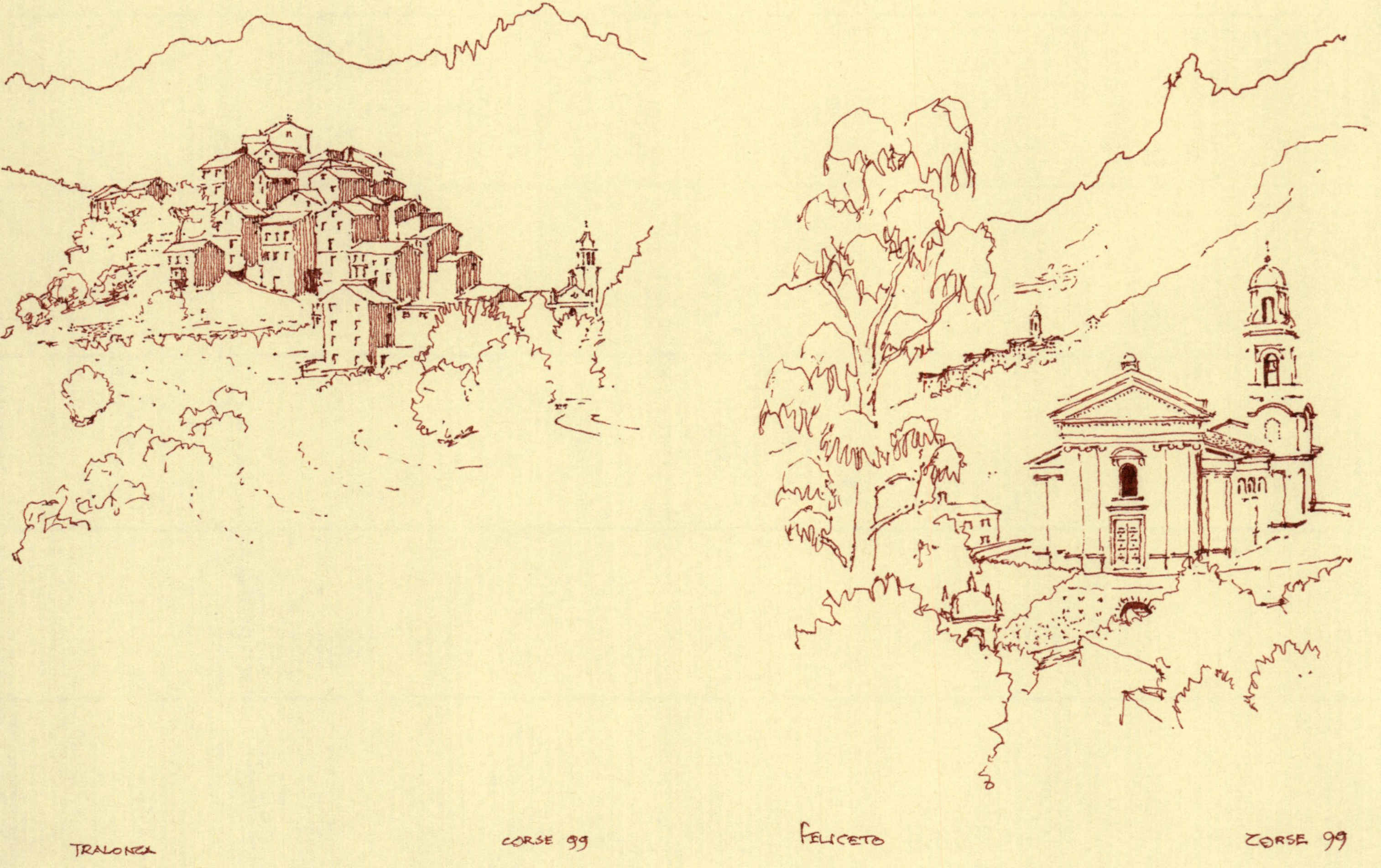
TRALONCA
CORSE 99
FELICETO
CORSE 99

GROSSA CORSE 99

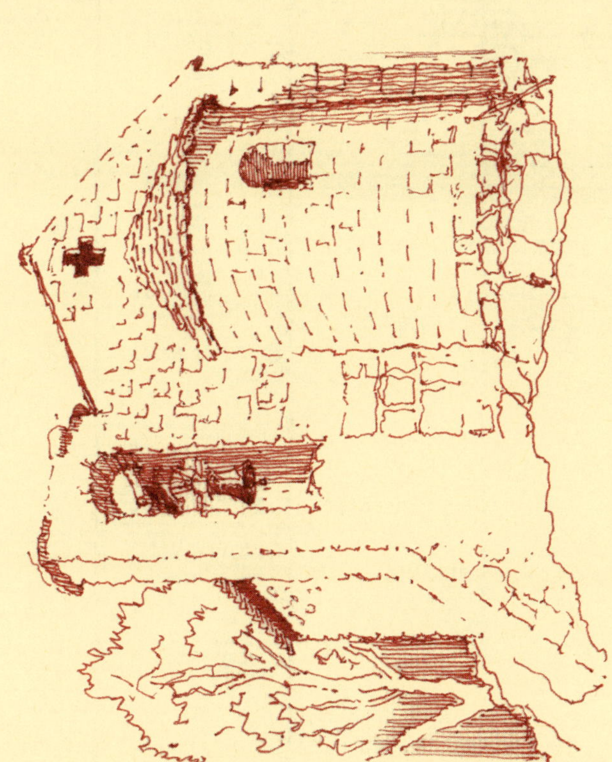

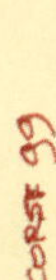

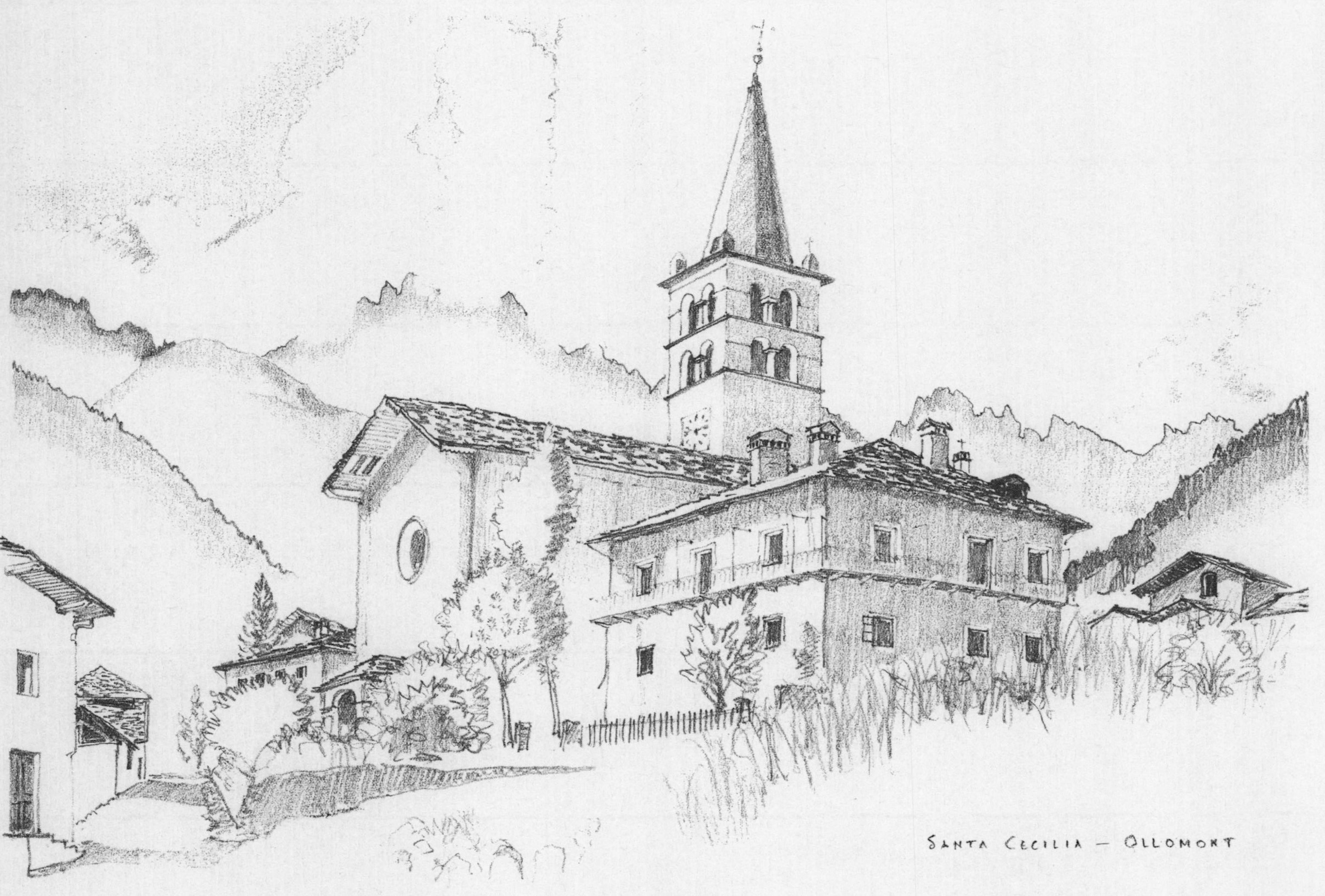

SANTA CECILIA — OLLOMONT

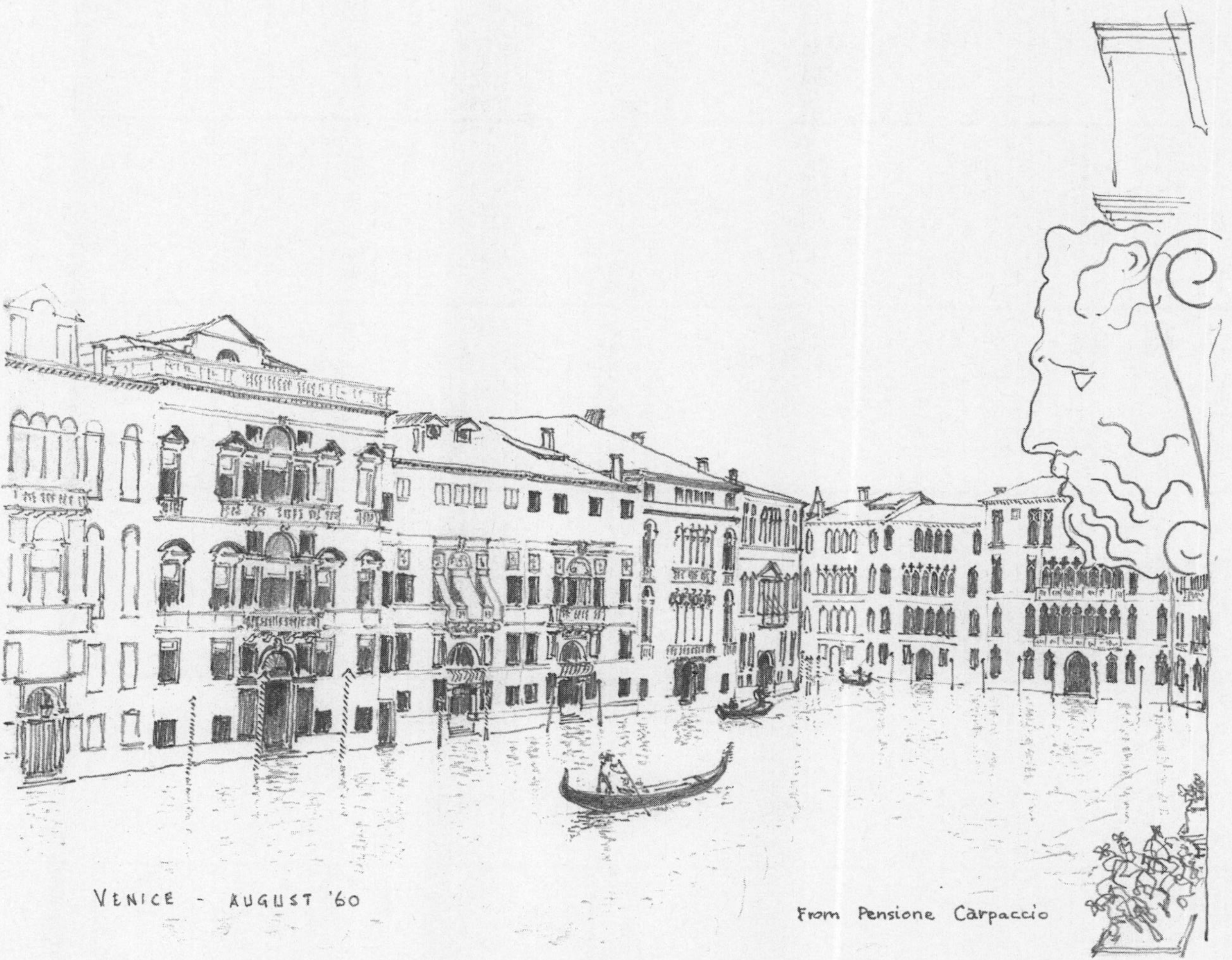
Venice - August '60
From Pensione Carpaccio

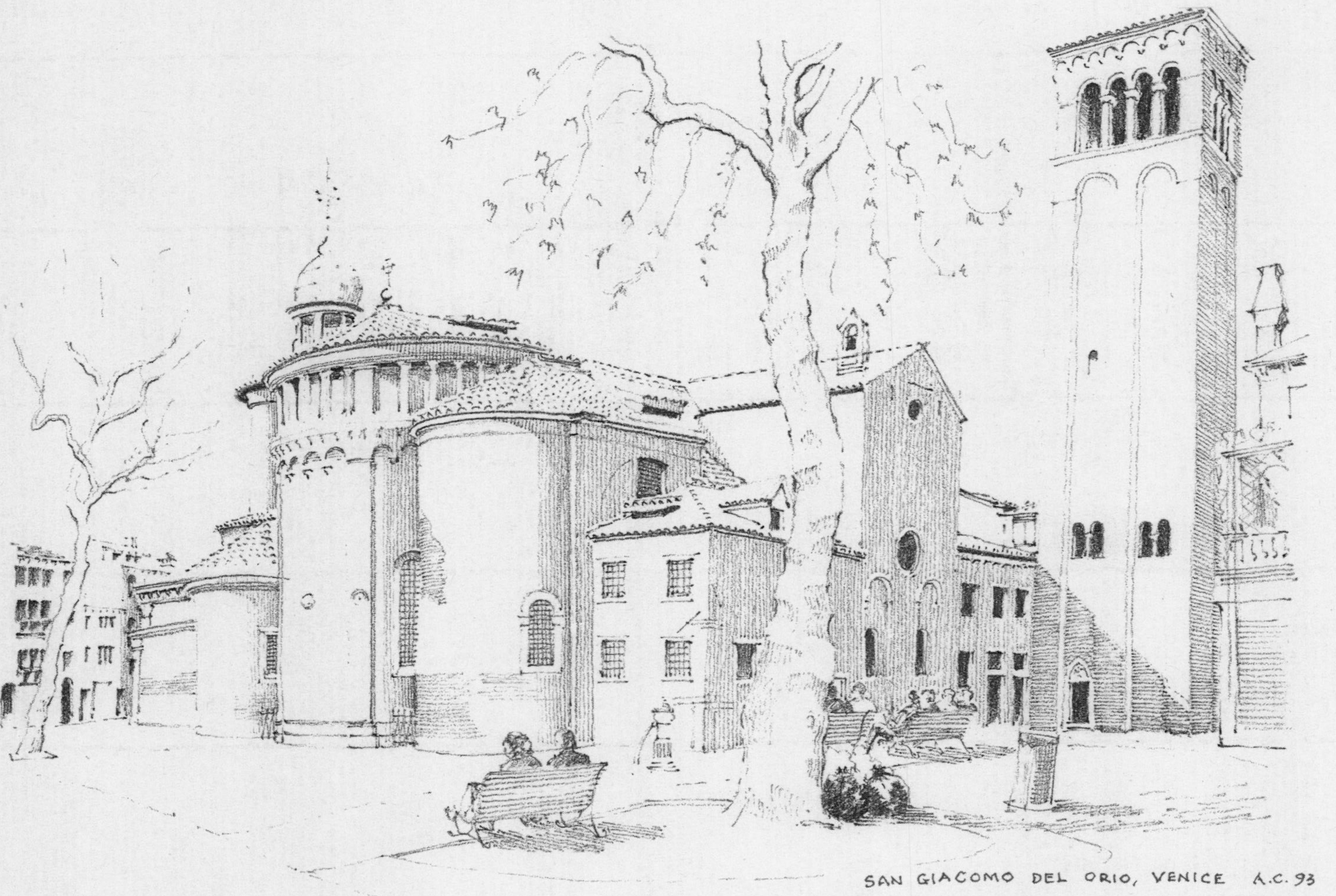

SAN GIACOMO DEL ORIO, VENICE A.C. 93

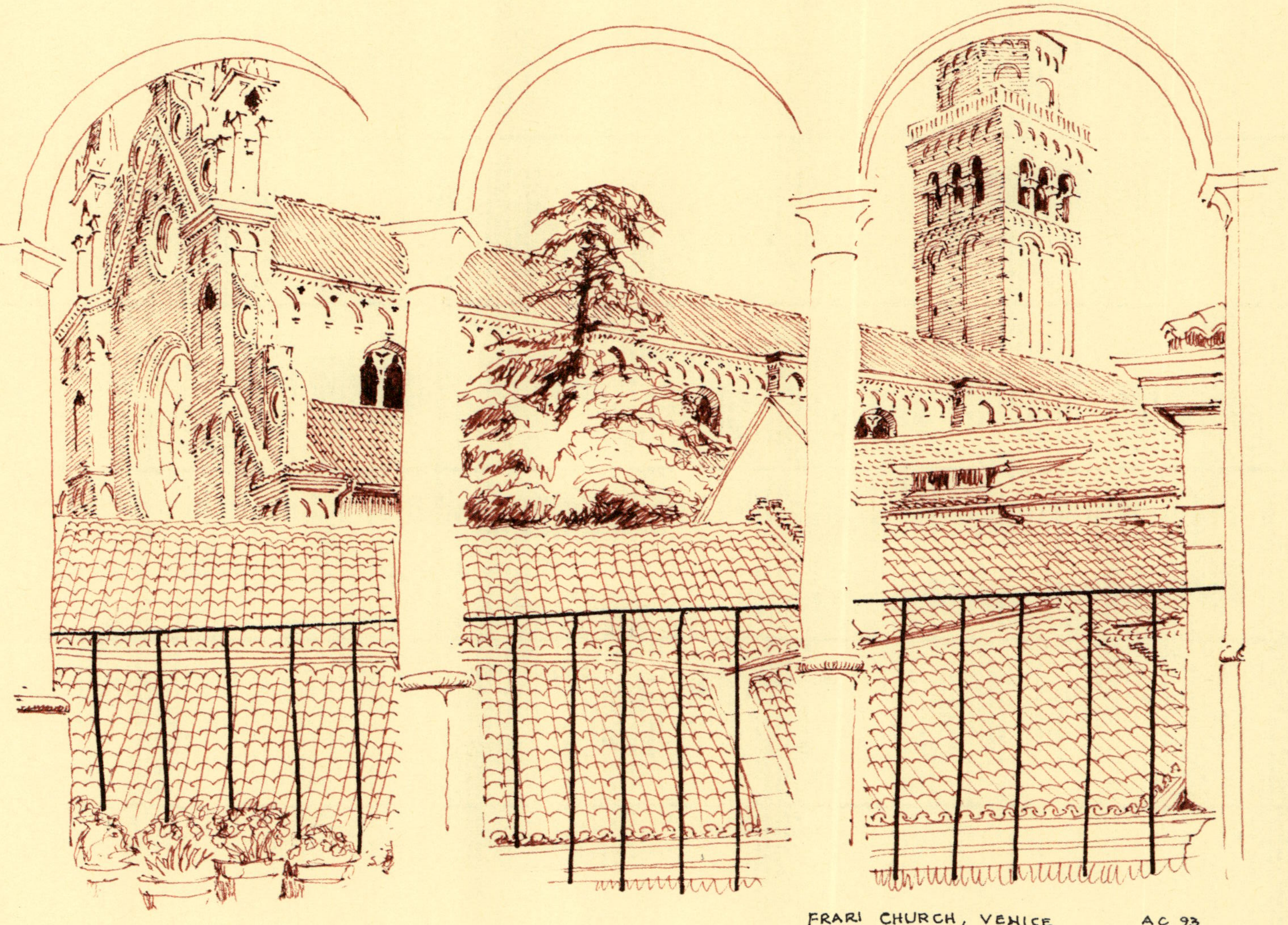
FRARI CHURCH, VENICE
AC 93

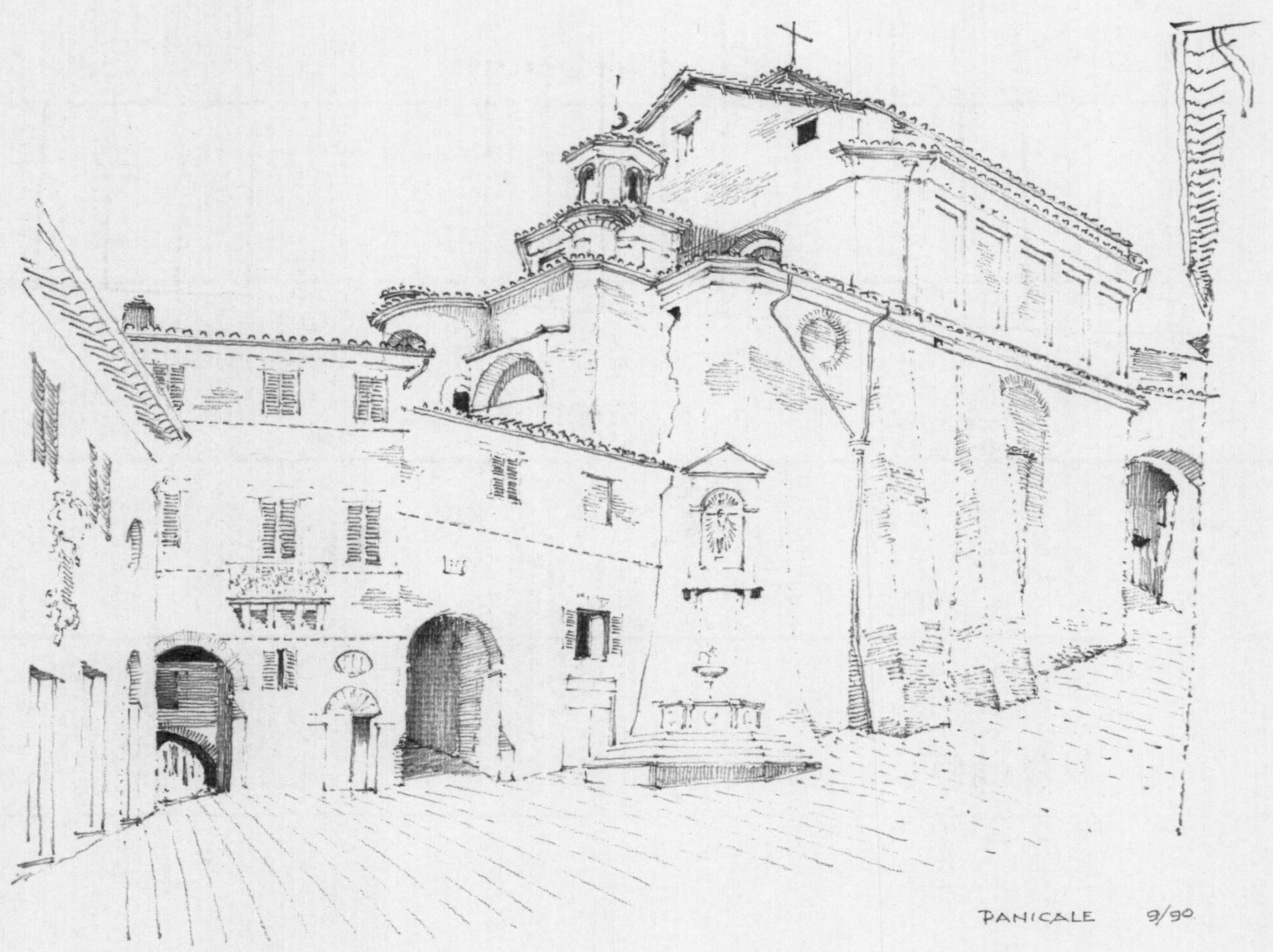
PANICALE
9/90

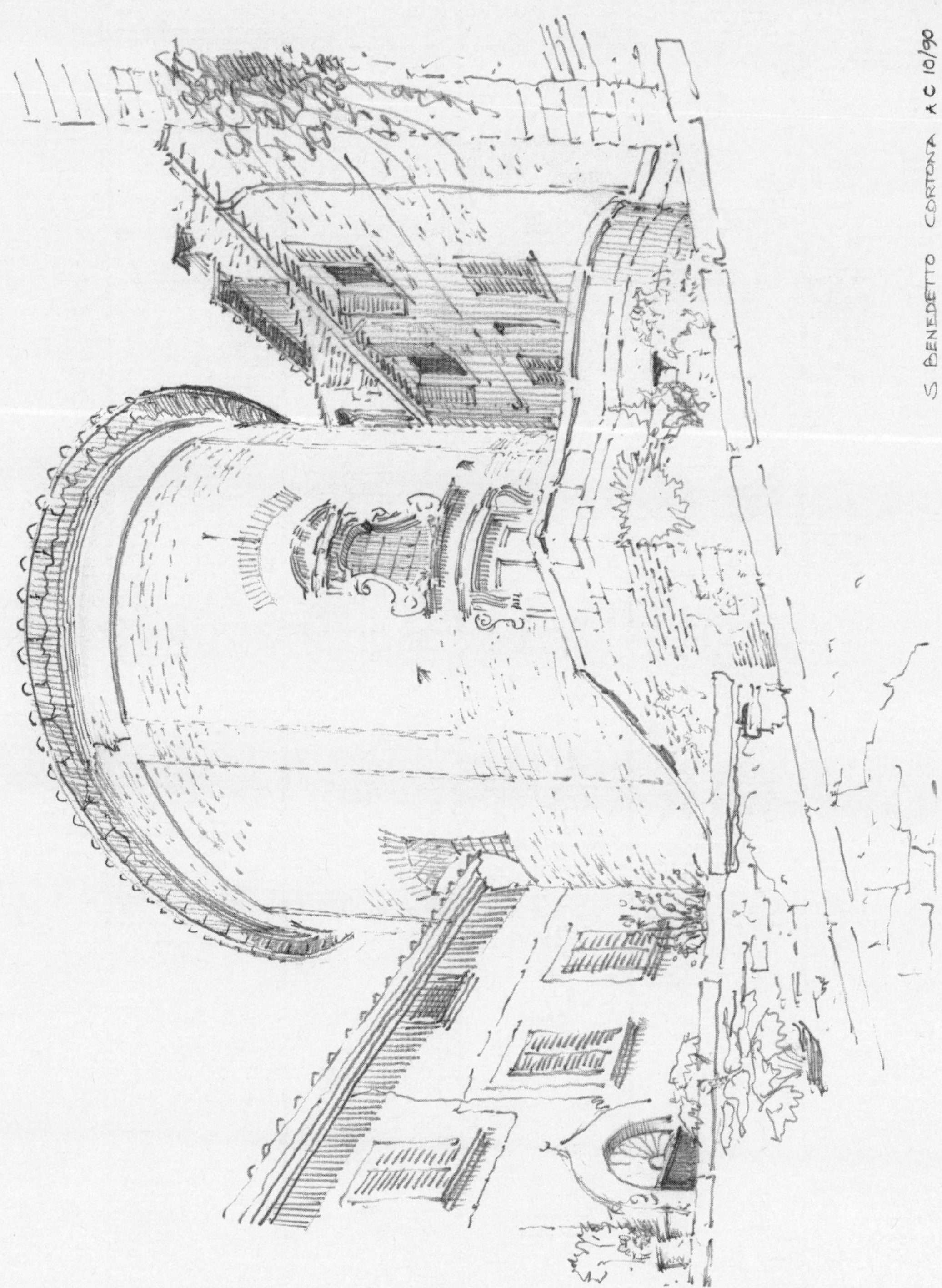
S BENEDETTO CORTONA AC 10/90

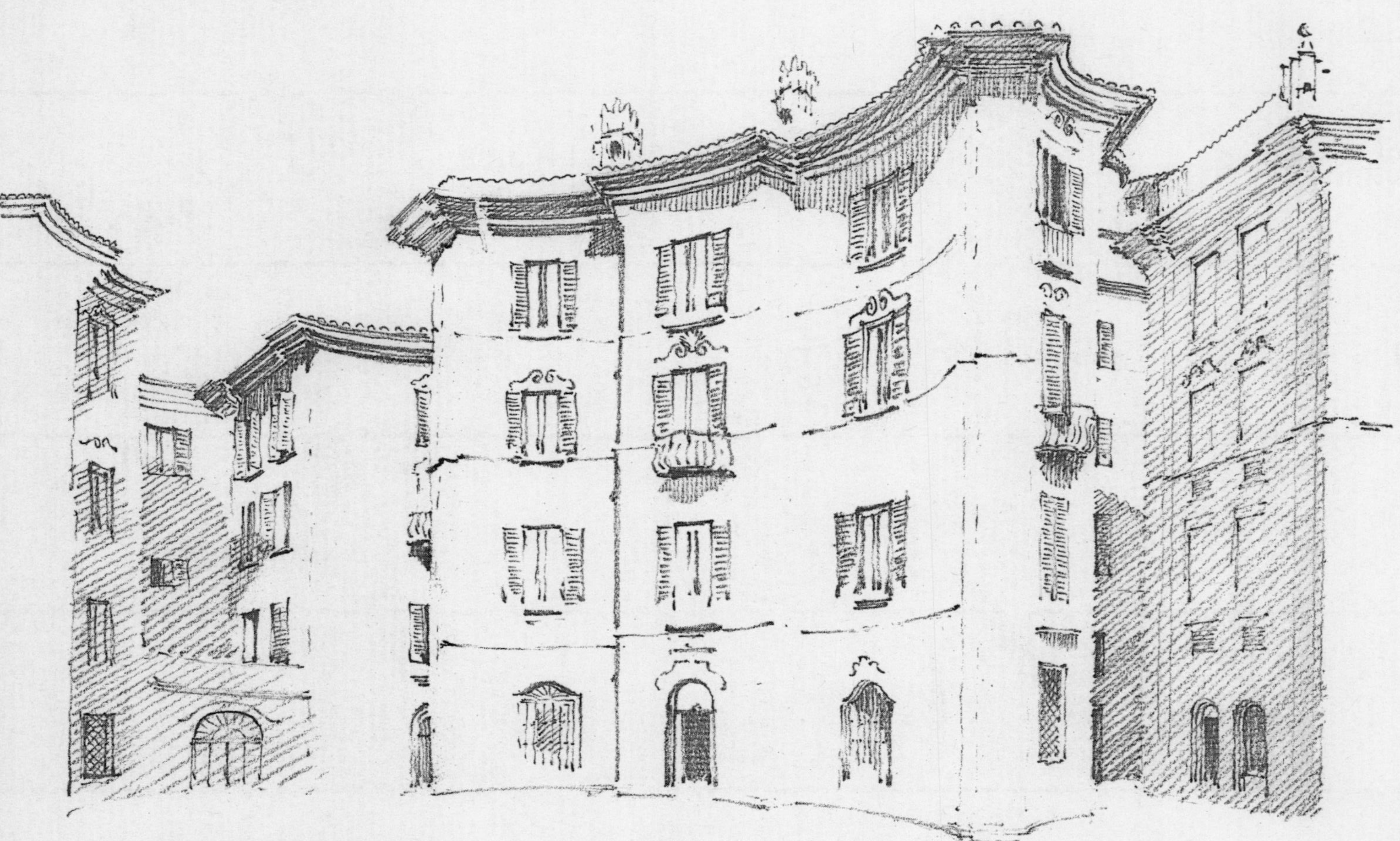

PIAZZA IGNAZIO, ROME
BY RAGUZZINI

When the Romans first drained the Pontine Marshes the inhabitants of hilltop NORBA moved down and built NINFA below complete with castle and four churches.

Decimated again by malaria in the Middle Ages the inhabitants abandoned Ninfa and moved back up to NORMA.

The Caetani family drained the marshes again for Mussolini and created this wonderful garden in the ruins.

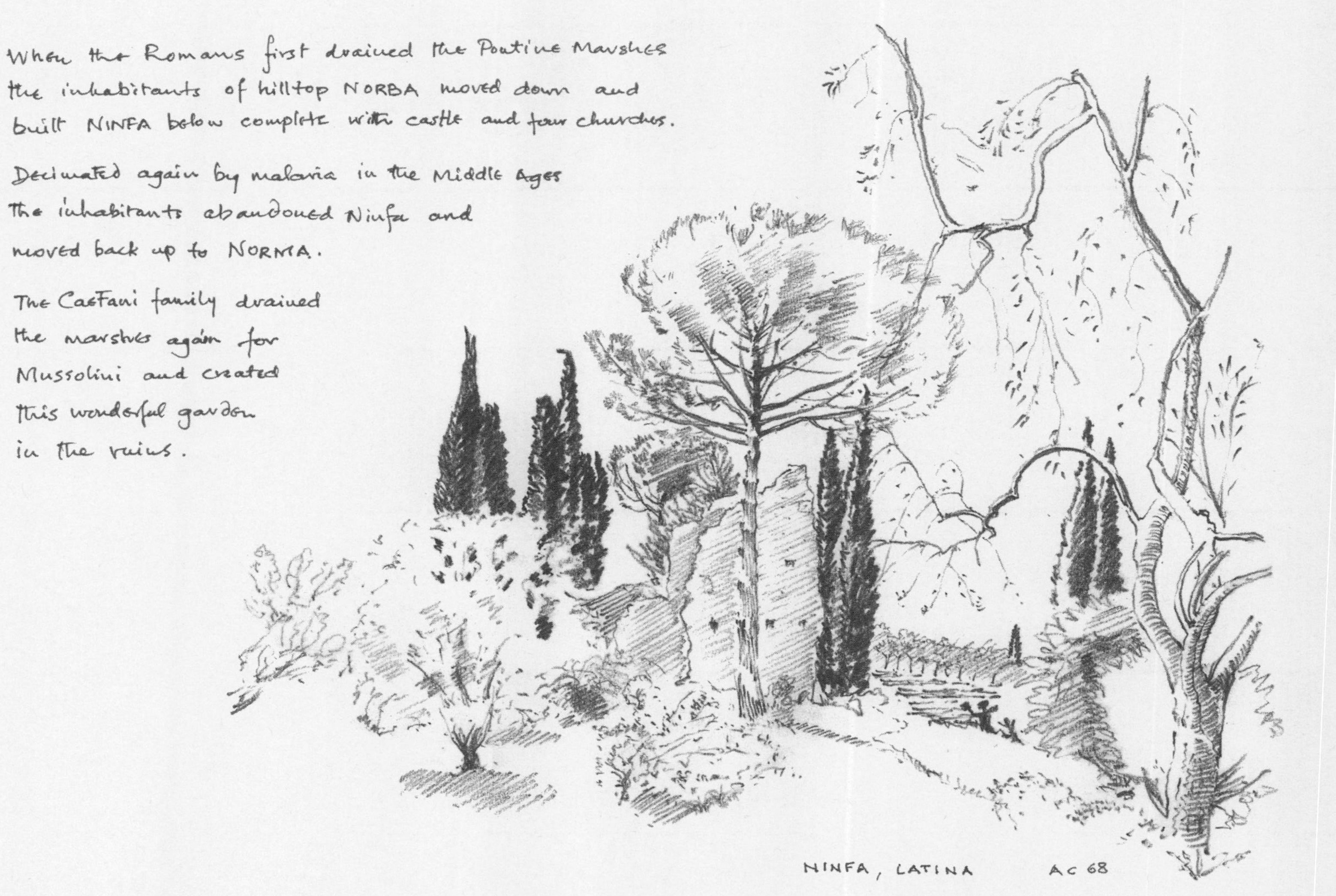

NINFA, LATINA   AC 68

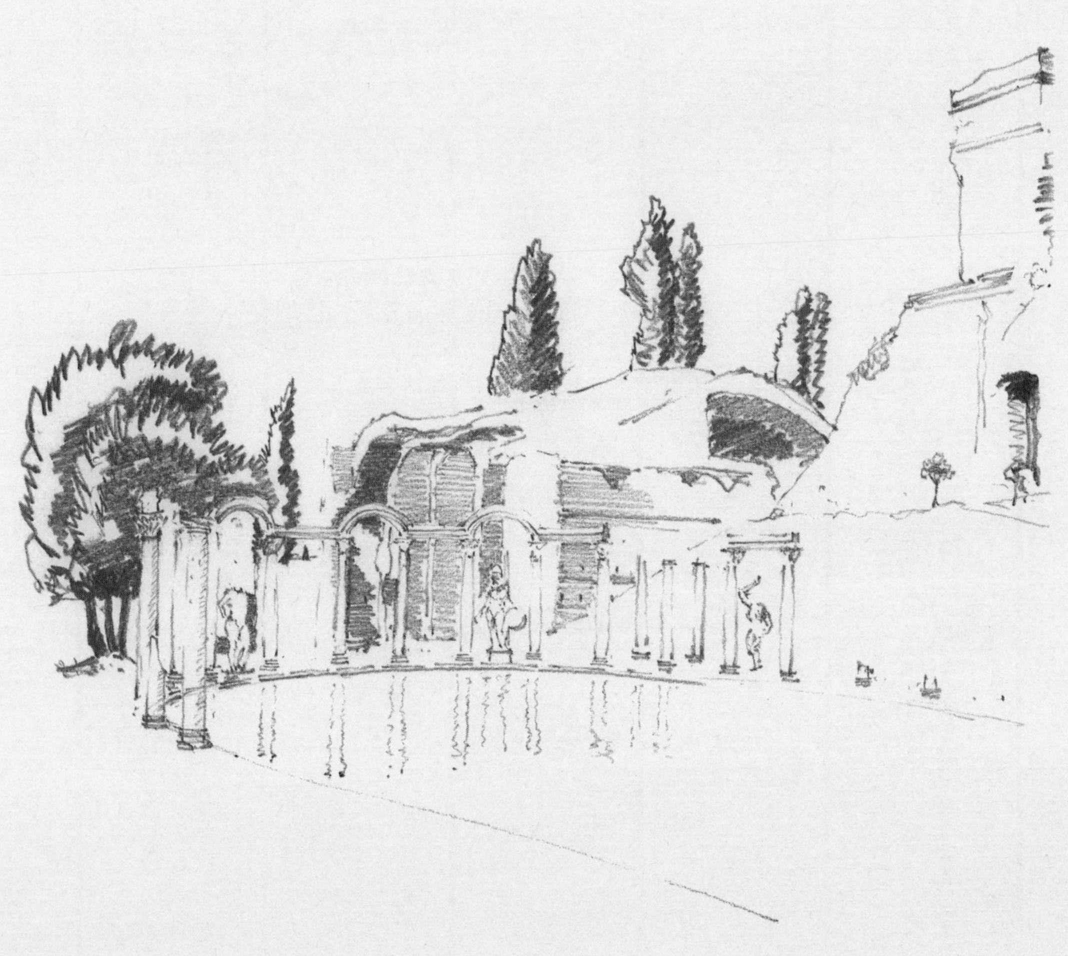

THE CANOPUS, HADRIAN'S VILLA, TIVOLI A.C. 68

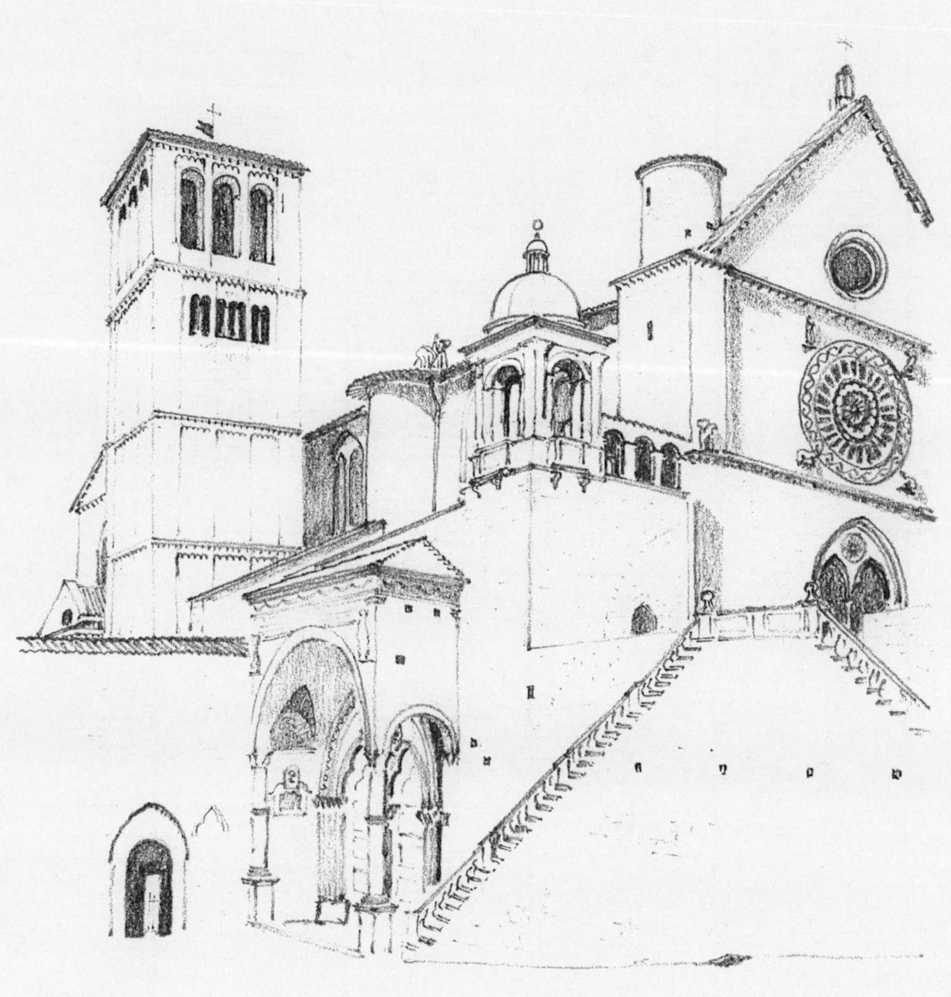

BASILICA OF ST FRANCIS - ASSISI

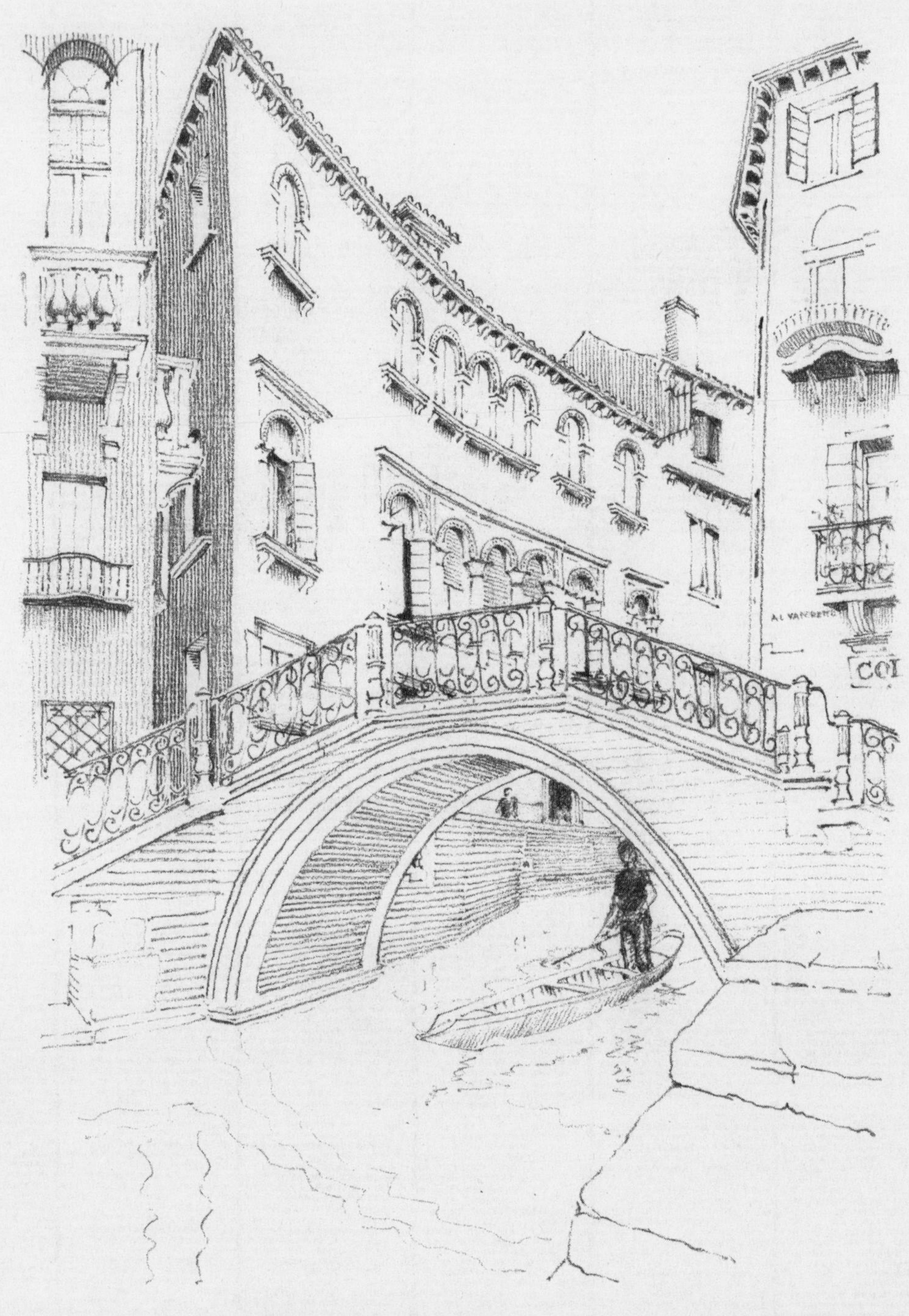

VENICE A.C. 93

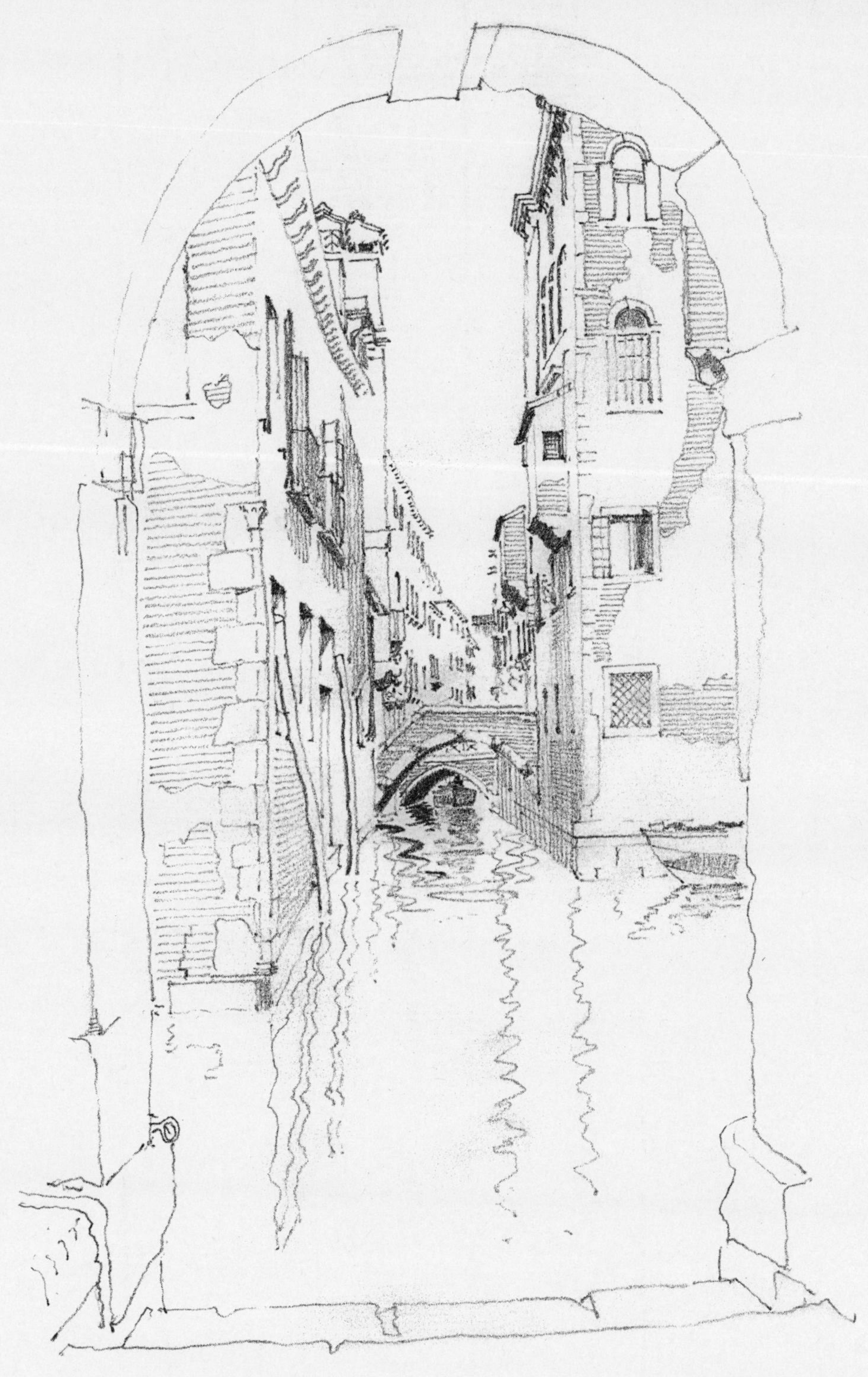

BOLDO CANAL, VENICE A.C. 93

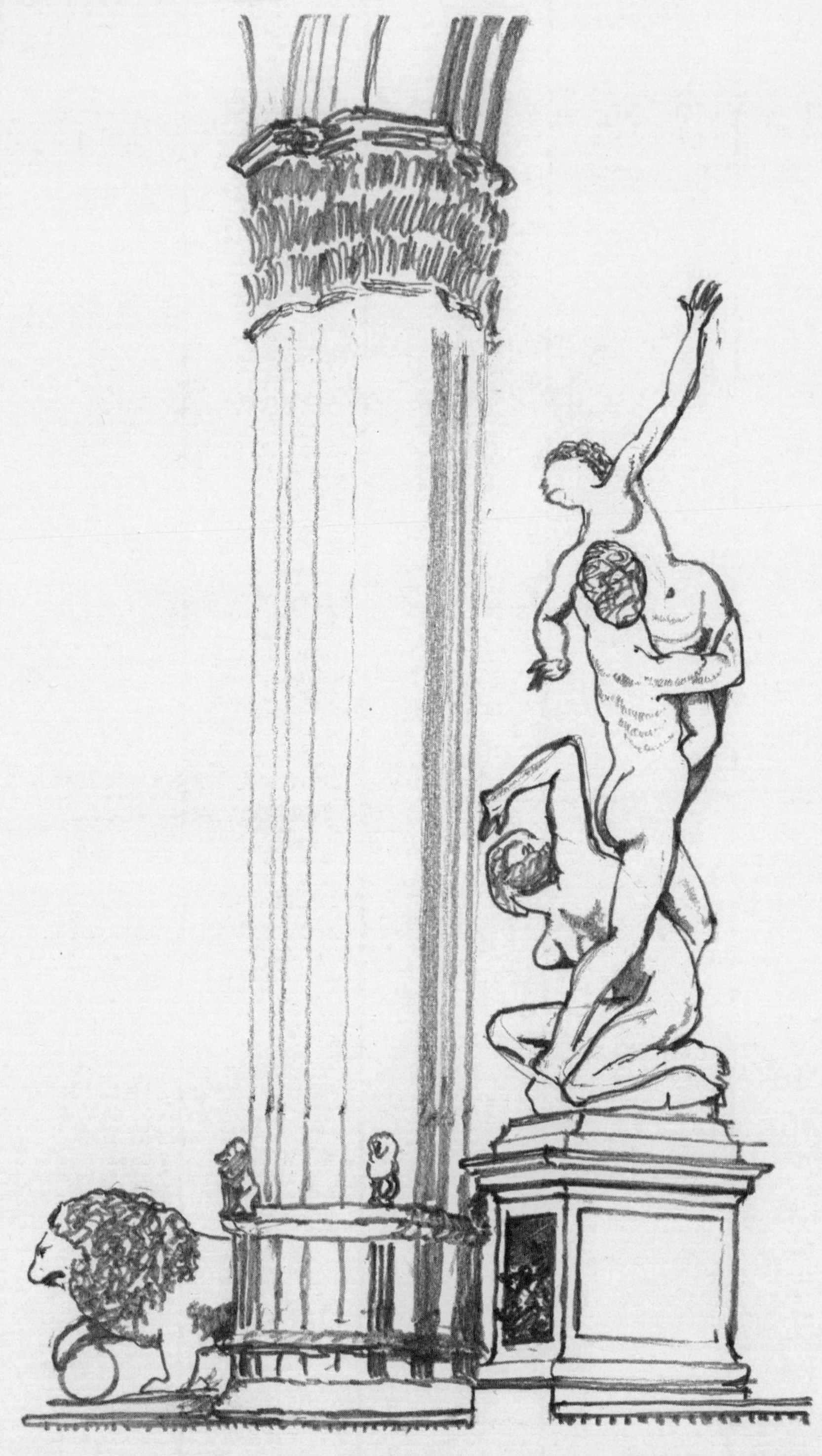

RAPE OF THE SABINES FLORENCE A.C. 57
(before Life Class)

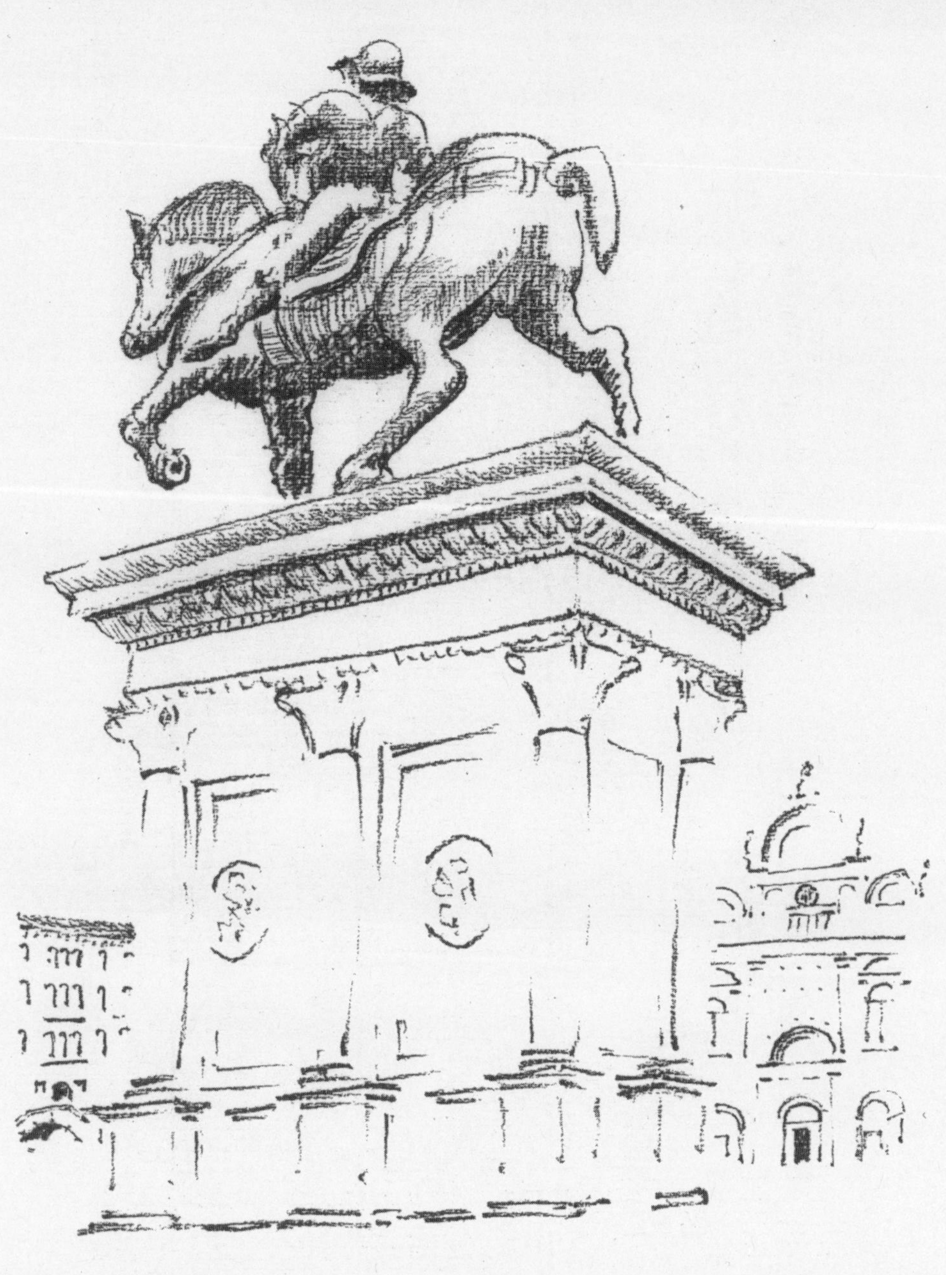
BARTOLOMEO COLLEONI
A.C.91
Near SCUOLA DI S MARCO (Right)

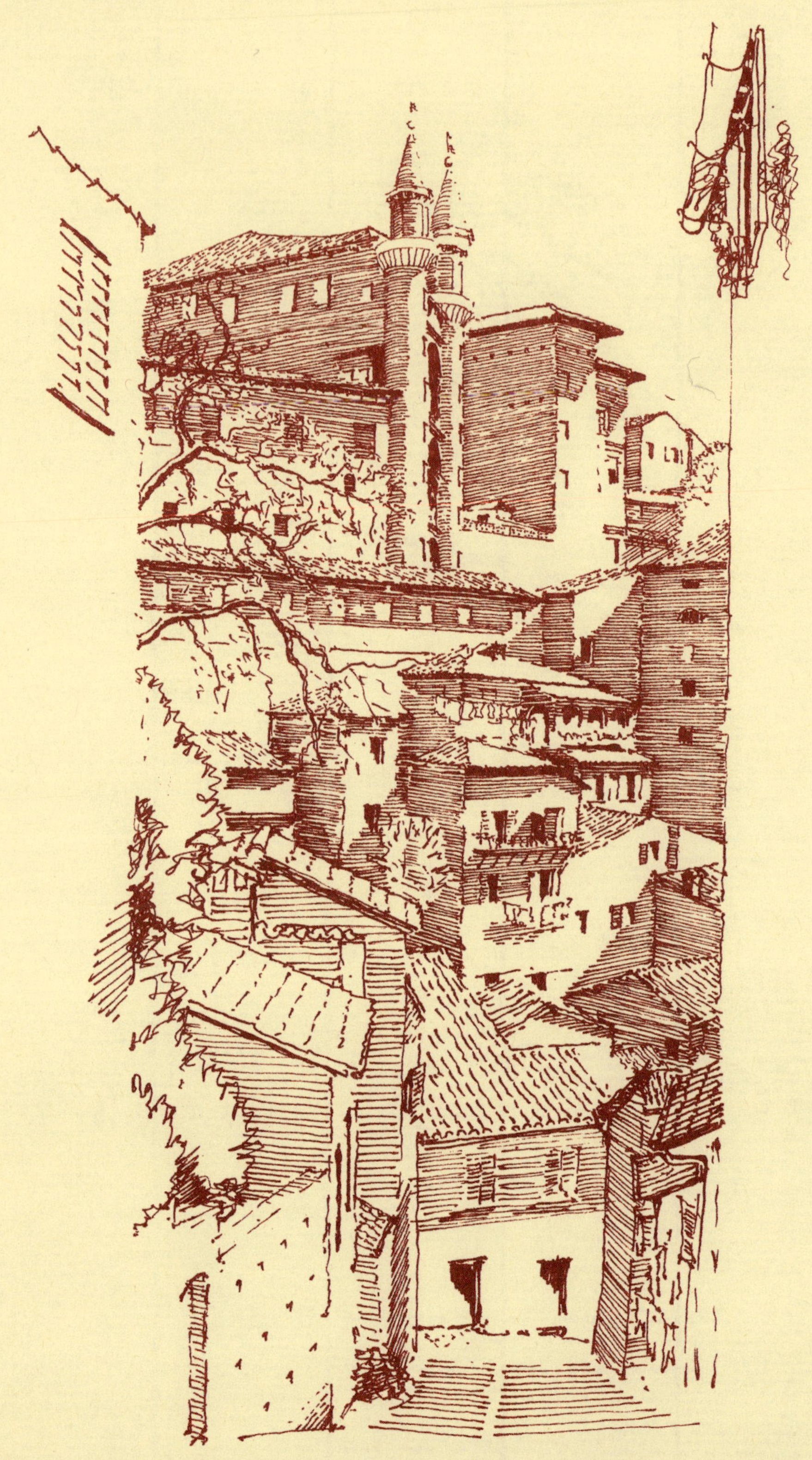

URBINO A.C. 78

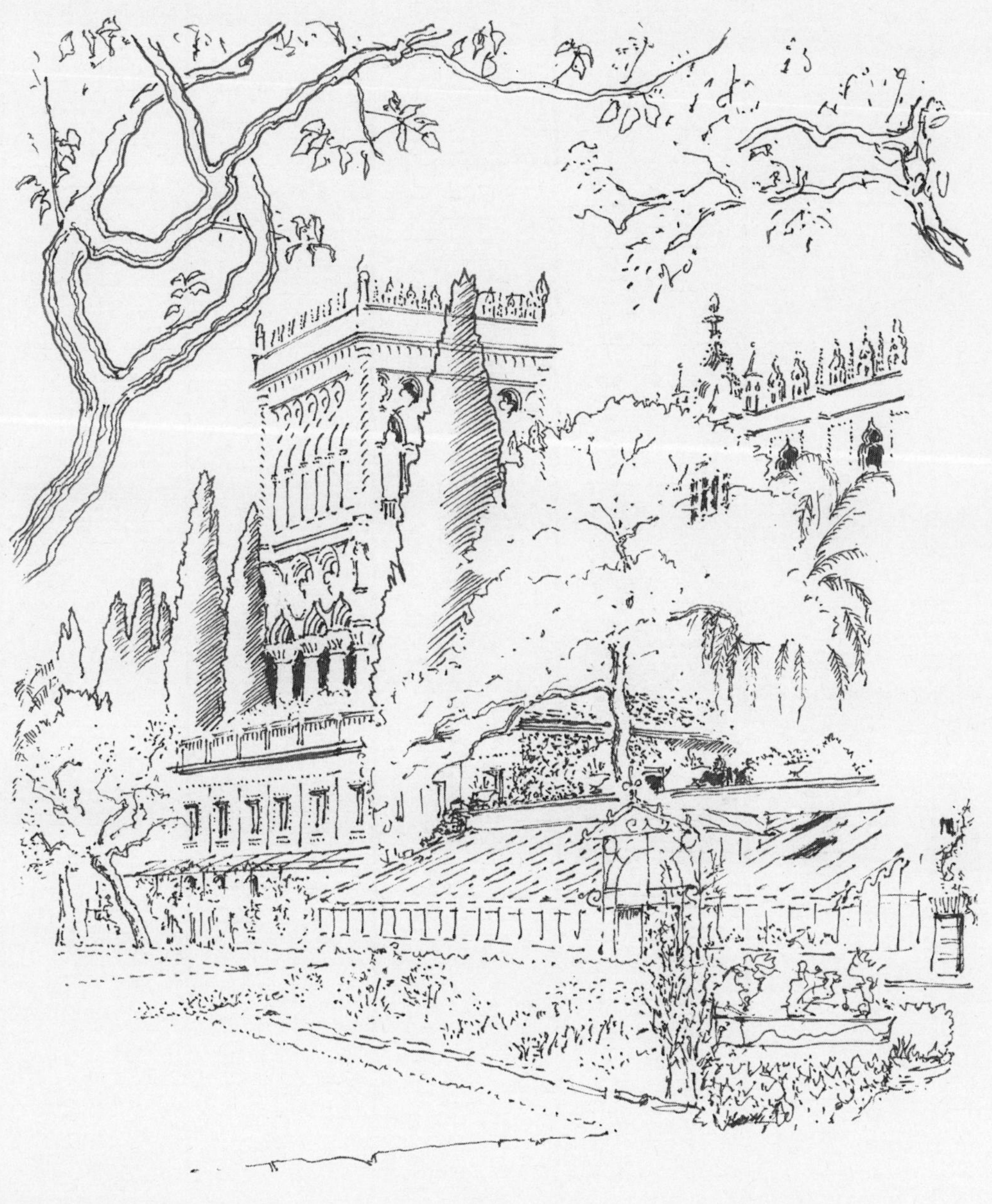

ISOLA DI GARDA AC84

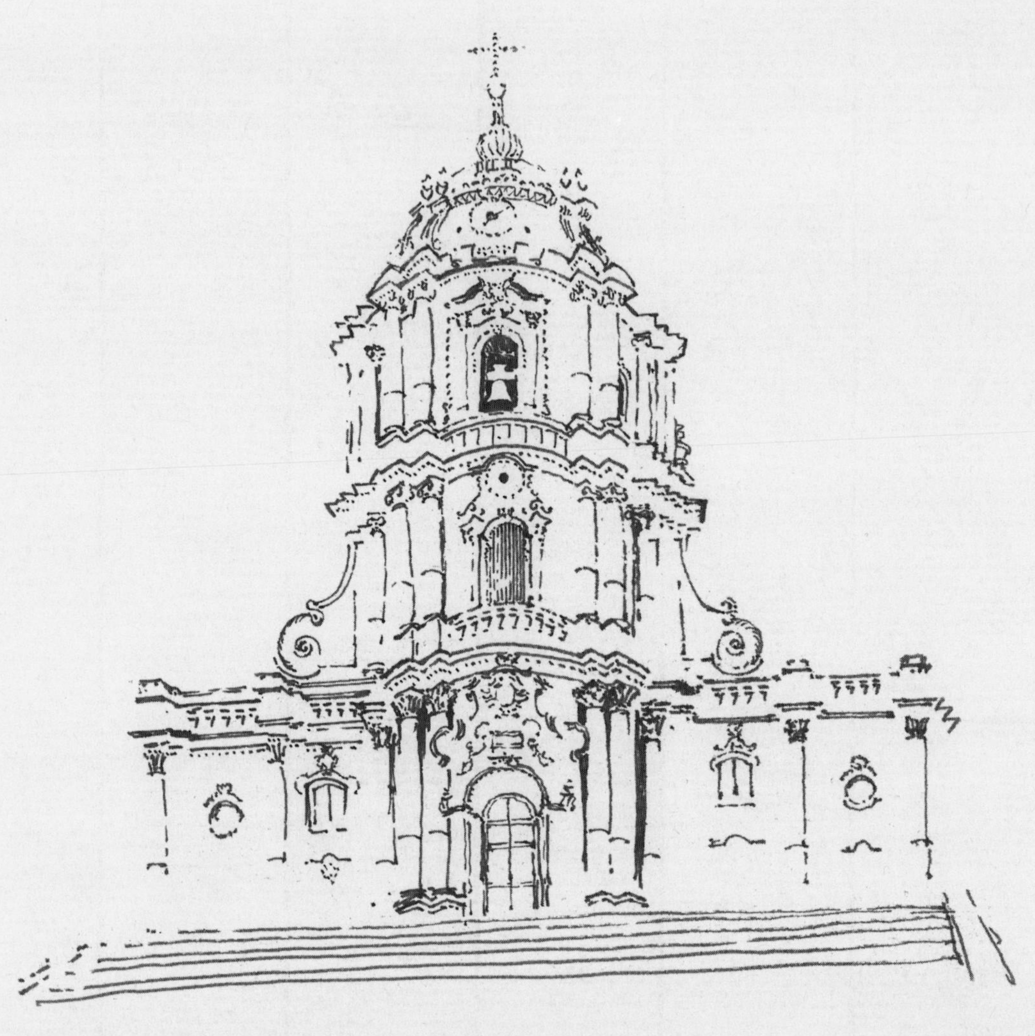

SAN GIORGIO MODICA - F.P. LABISI AC 74

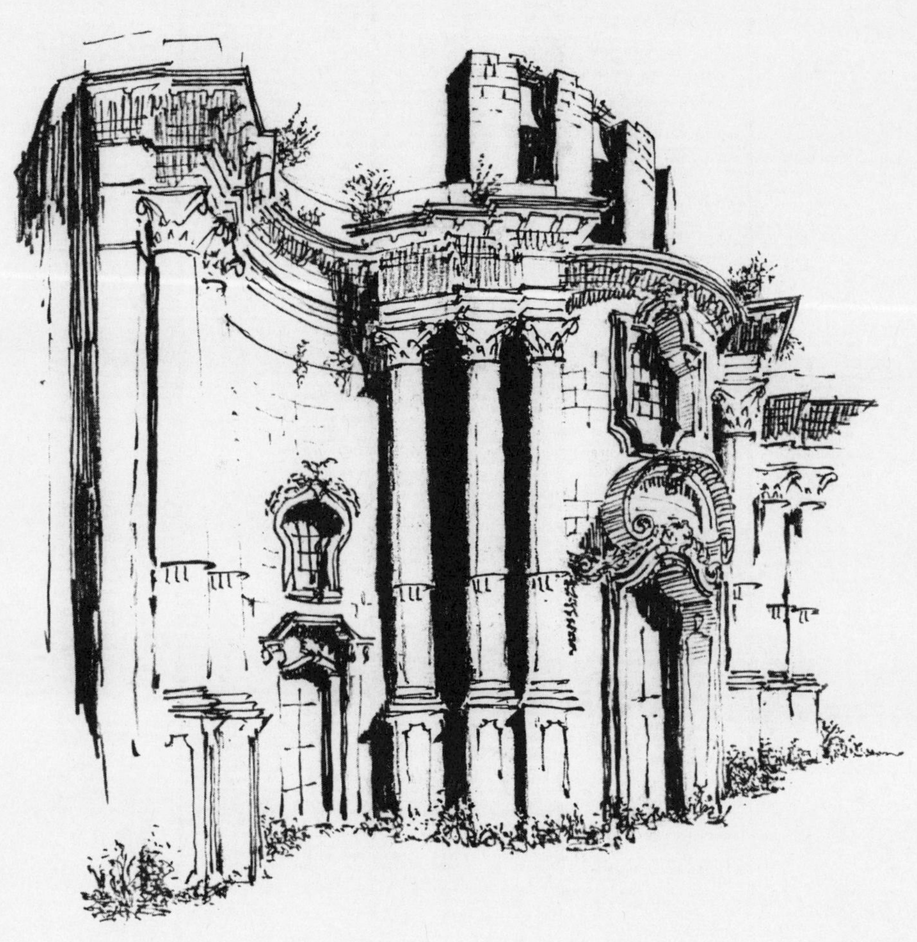

SAN ANTONIO, BUSCEMI - GAGLIARDI? A C 83

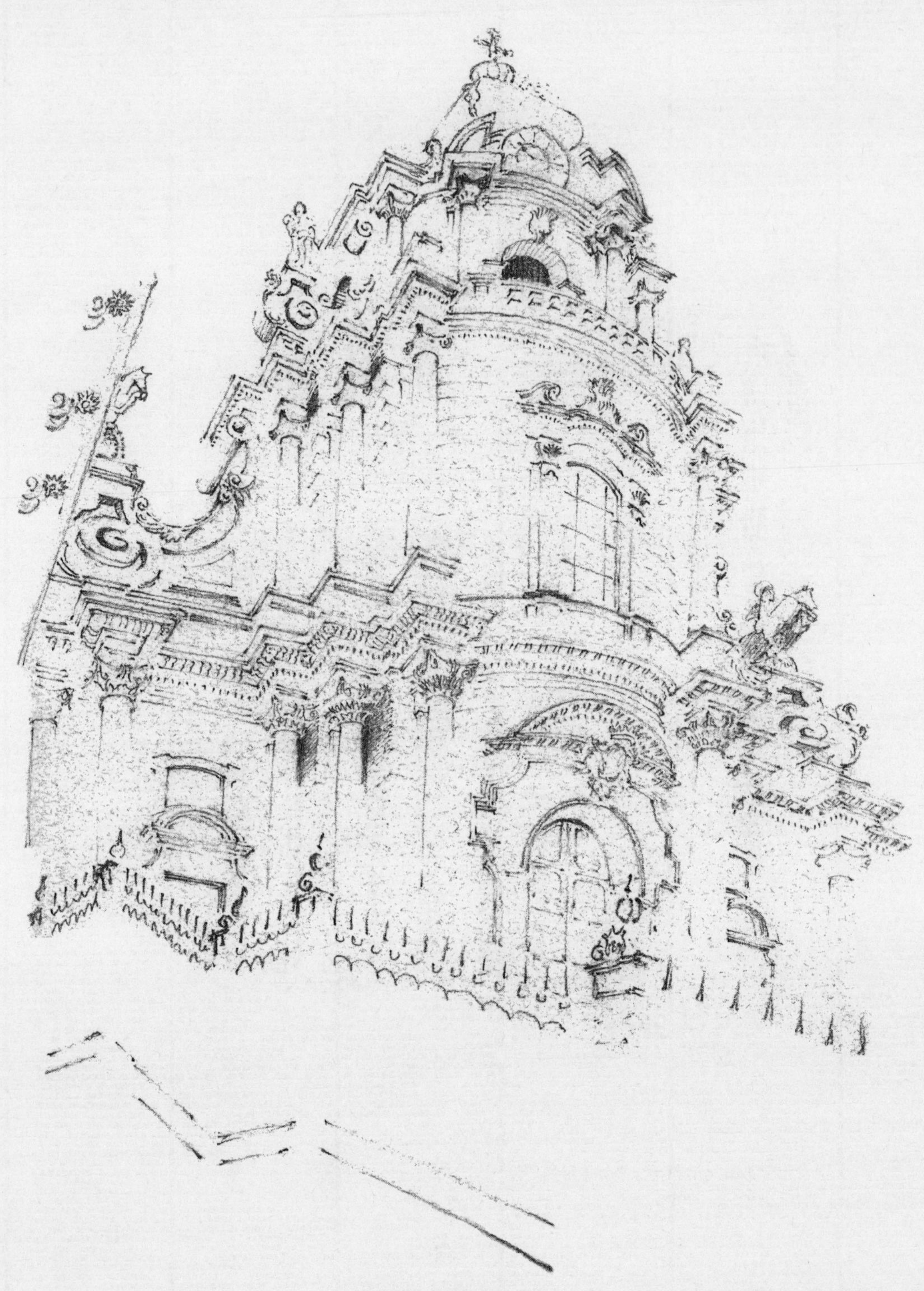

SAN GIORGIO, RAGUSA IBLA – GAGLIARDI A.C. 77

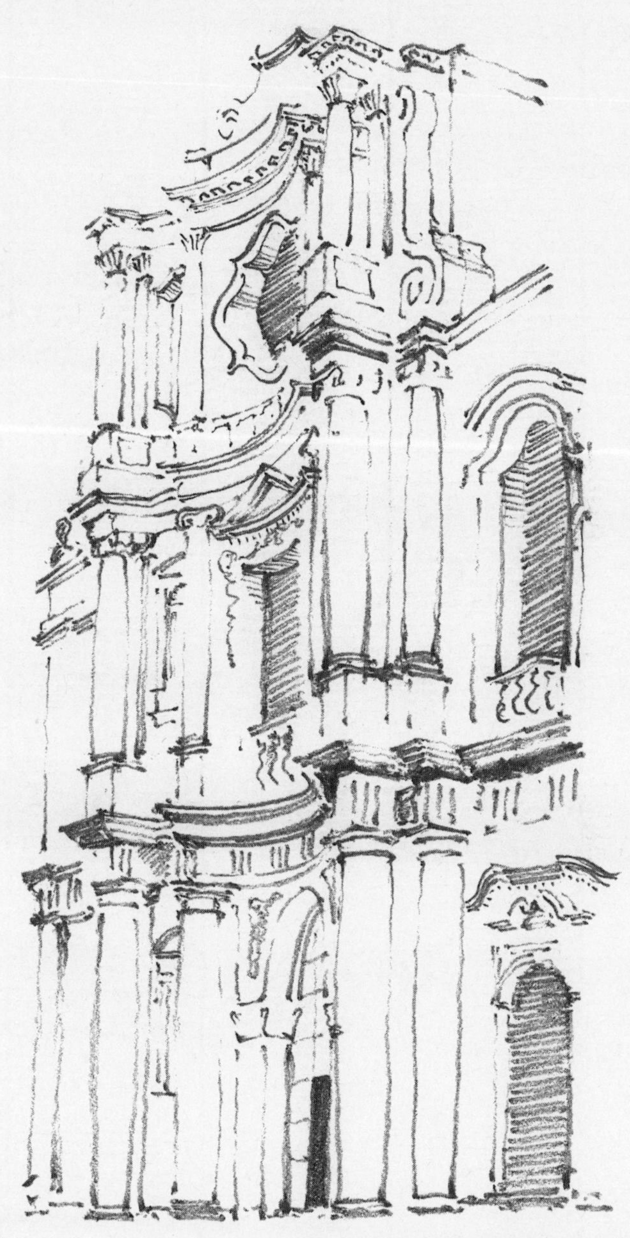

CHIESA DEL COLLEGIO DA SAN CARLO, NOTO A.C.74

It was Sarah Mathieson who persuaded Alvin Boyarsky to take on this 54 year old 'student' on the strength of this drawing.

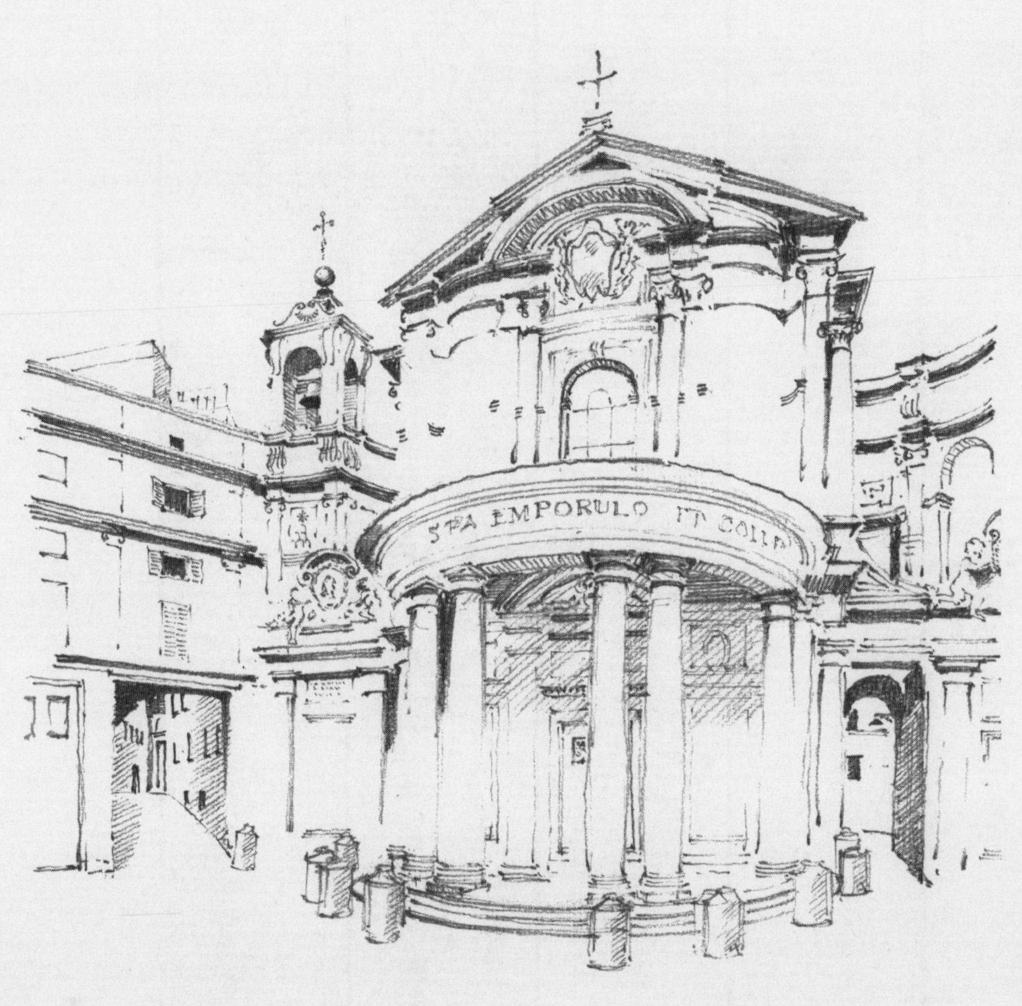

STA. MARIA DELLA PACE (PIETRO DA CORTONA) ROME

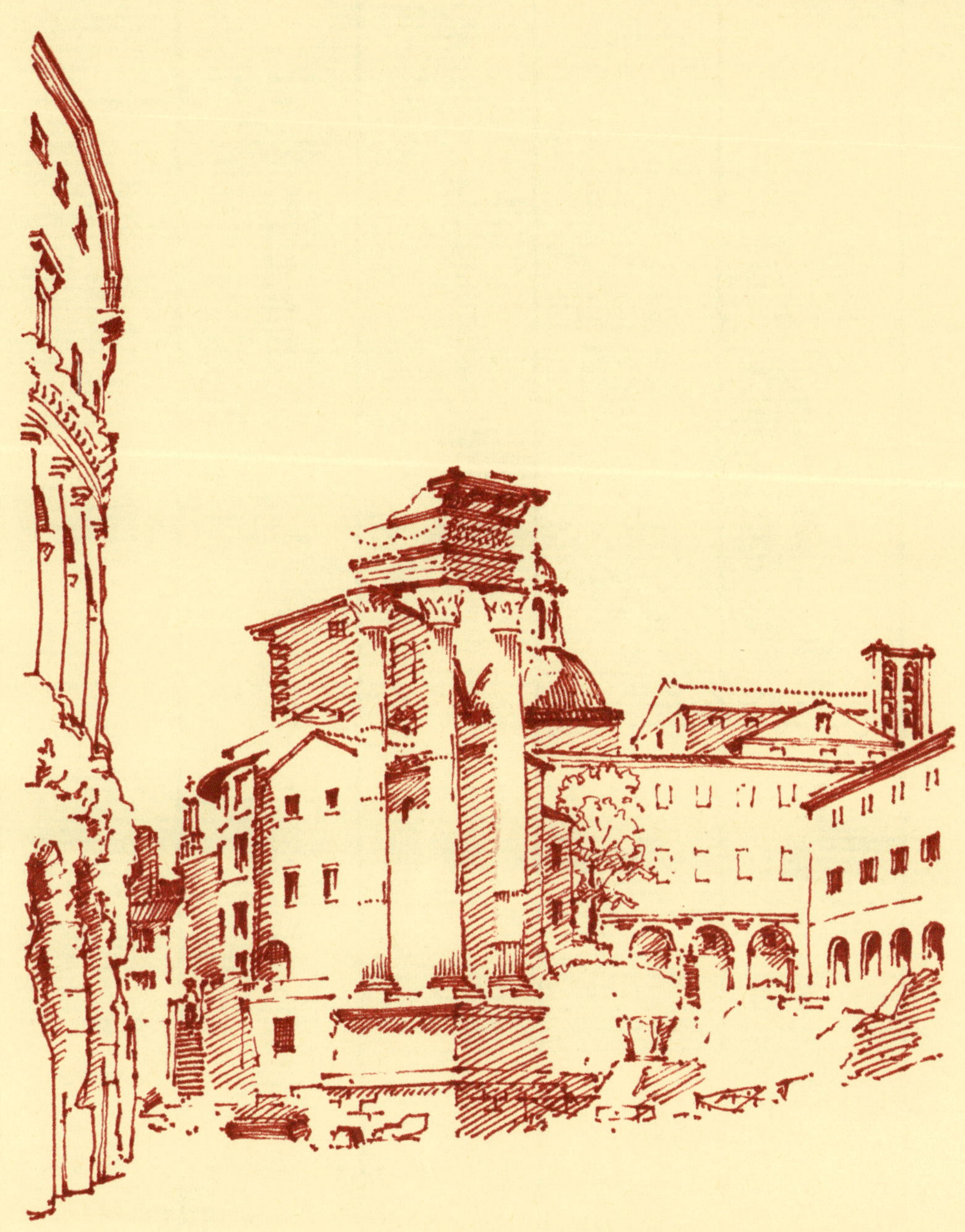

MARCELLUS THEATRE ROME

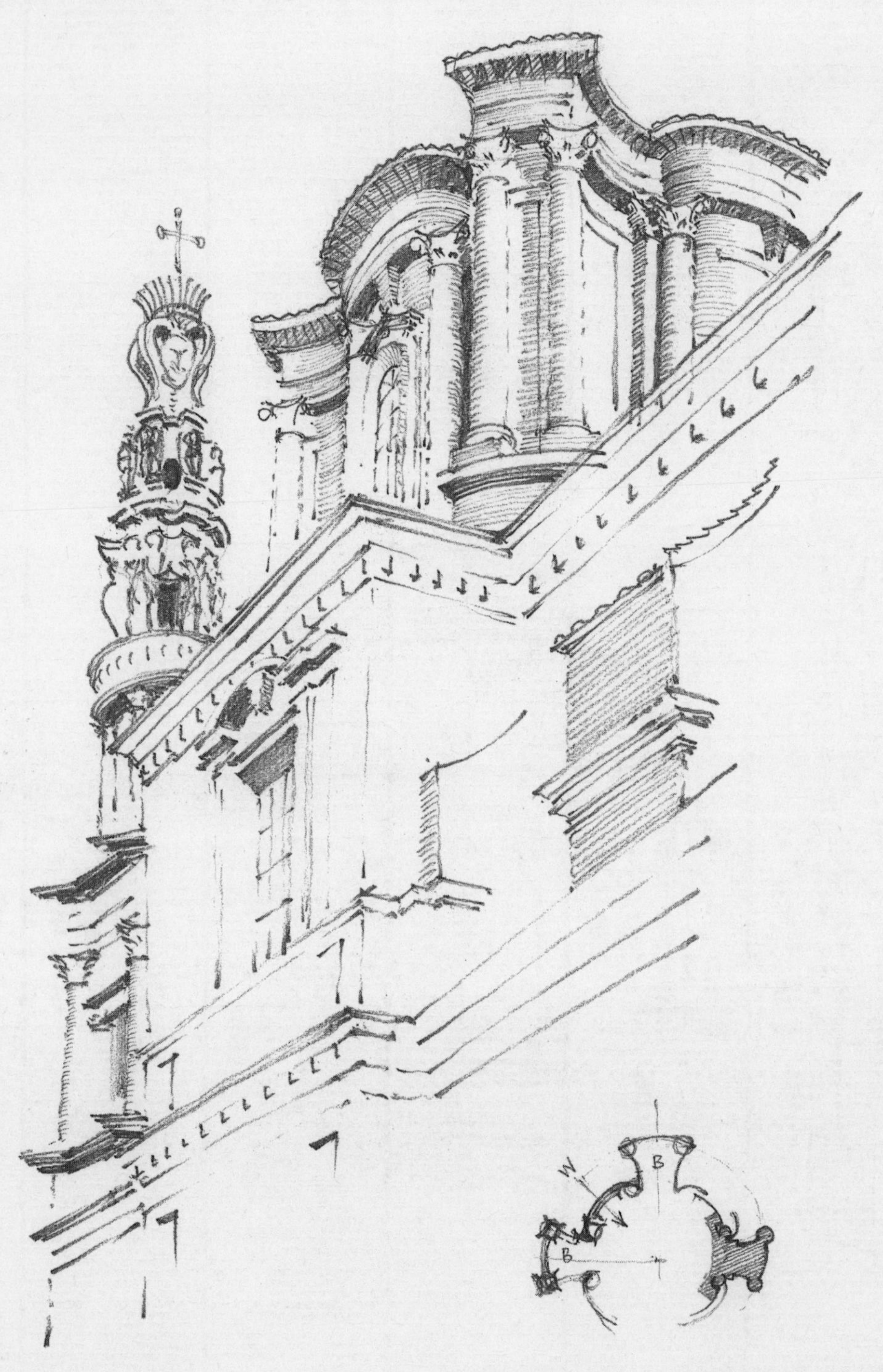

SAN ANDREA DELLE FRATTE, ROME BY BORROMINI WHICH NEVER GOT ITS DOME OF HIS DESIGN A.C. 81

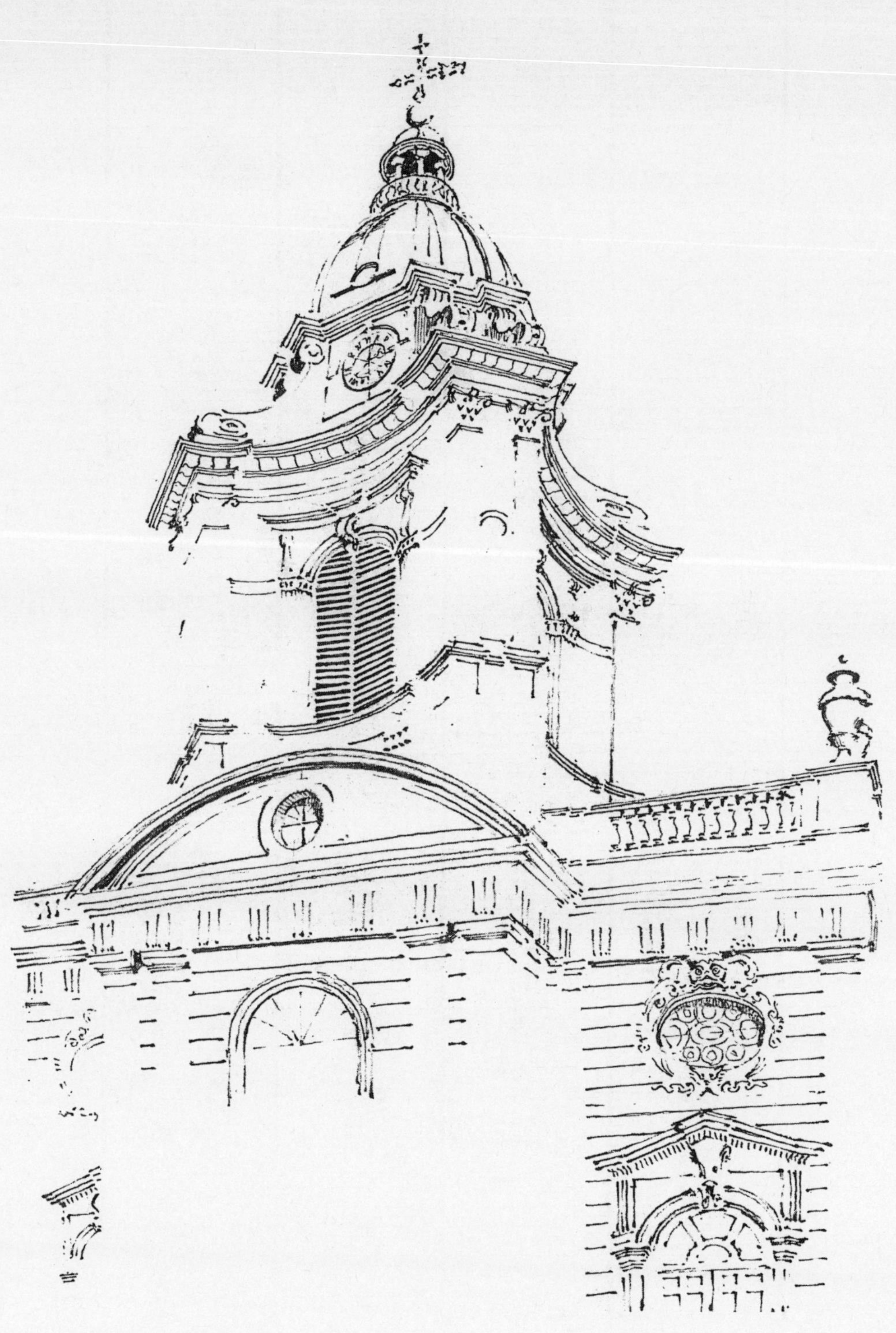

ST. PHILIP, BIRMINGHAM BY THOMAS ARCHER WHO VISITED ROME AND POSSIBLY ALSO BORROMINI WHEN THE FRATTE WAS UNDER CONSTRUCTION. A.C.82

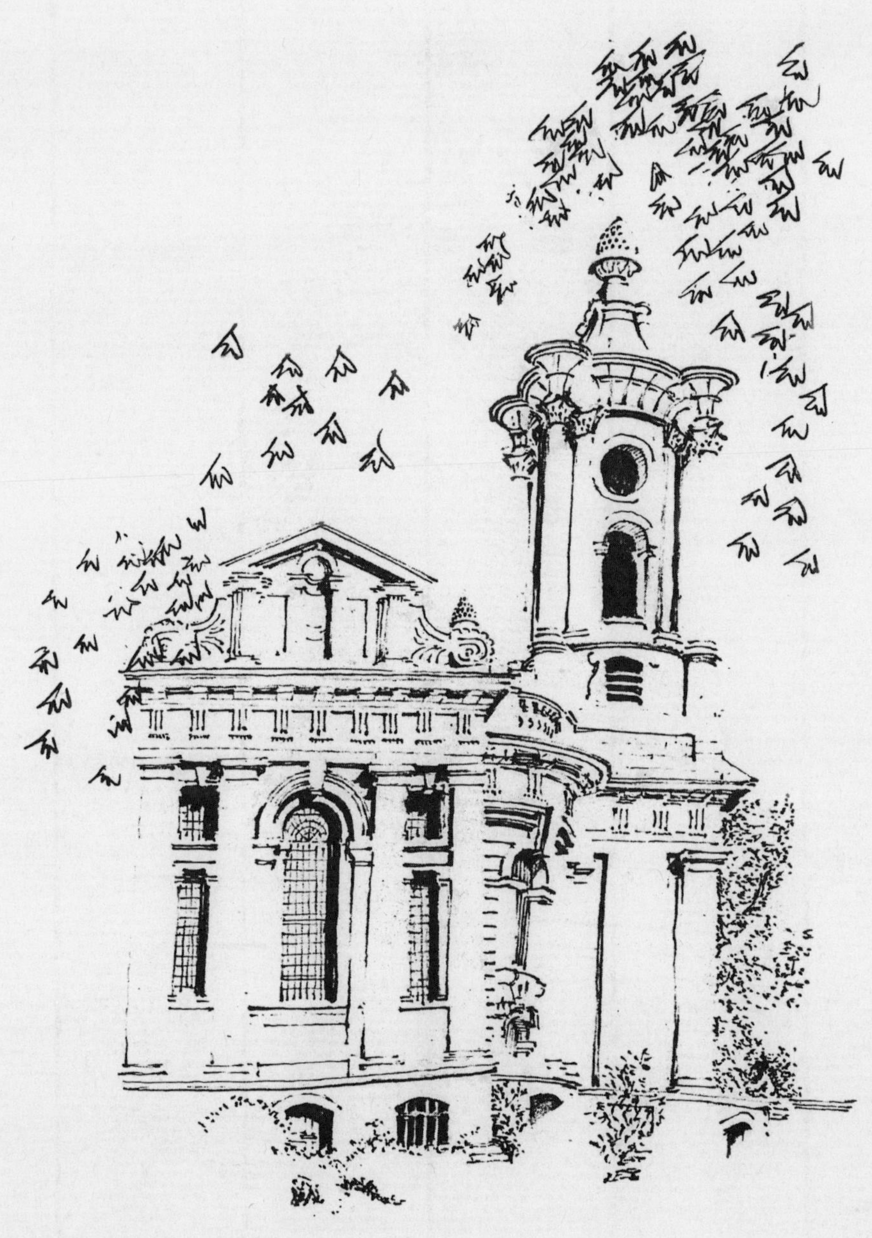

ST. JOHN, SMITH SQUARE BY THOMAS ARCHER A.C. 80

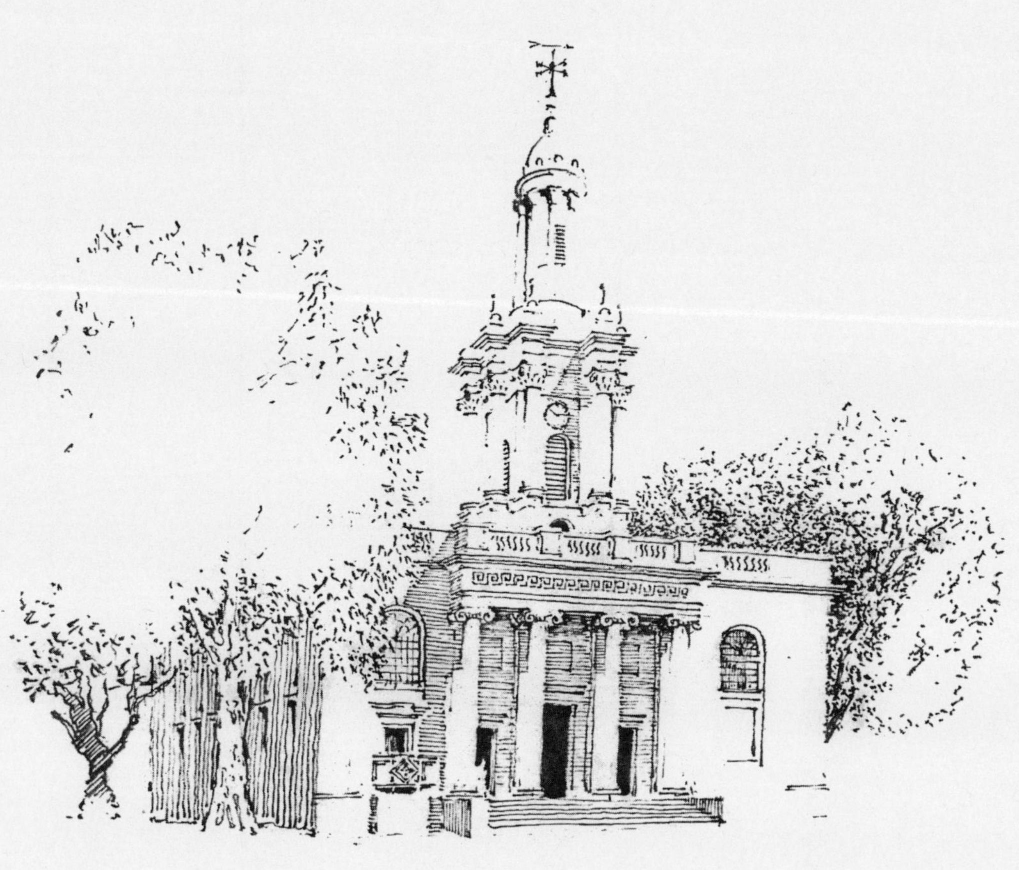

HOLY TRINITY, MARYLEBONE BY SOANE

A.C. 80

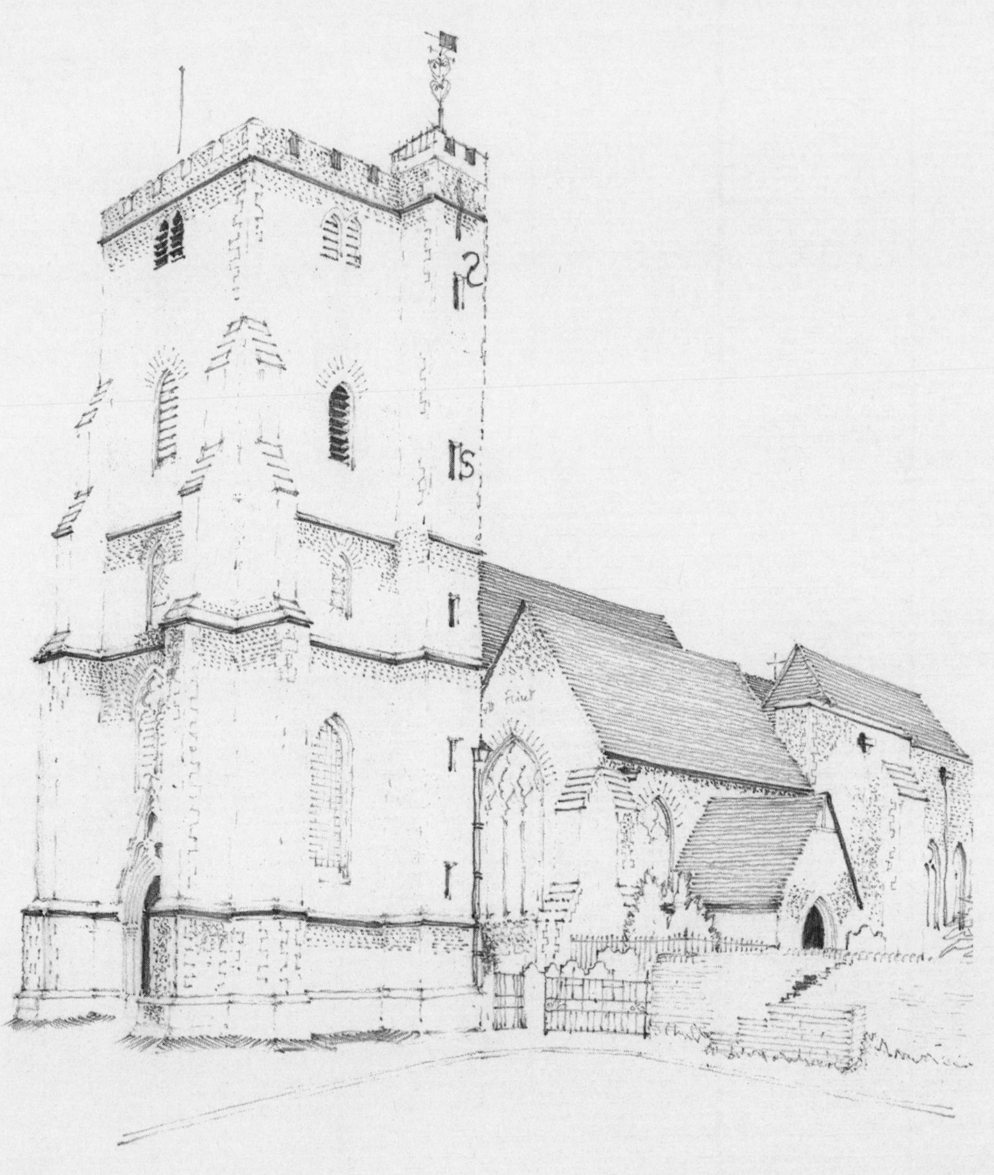

MILTON REGIS A.C. 85

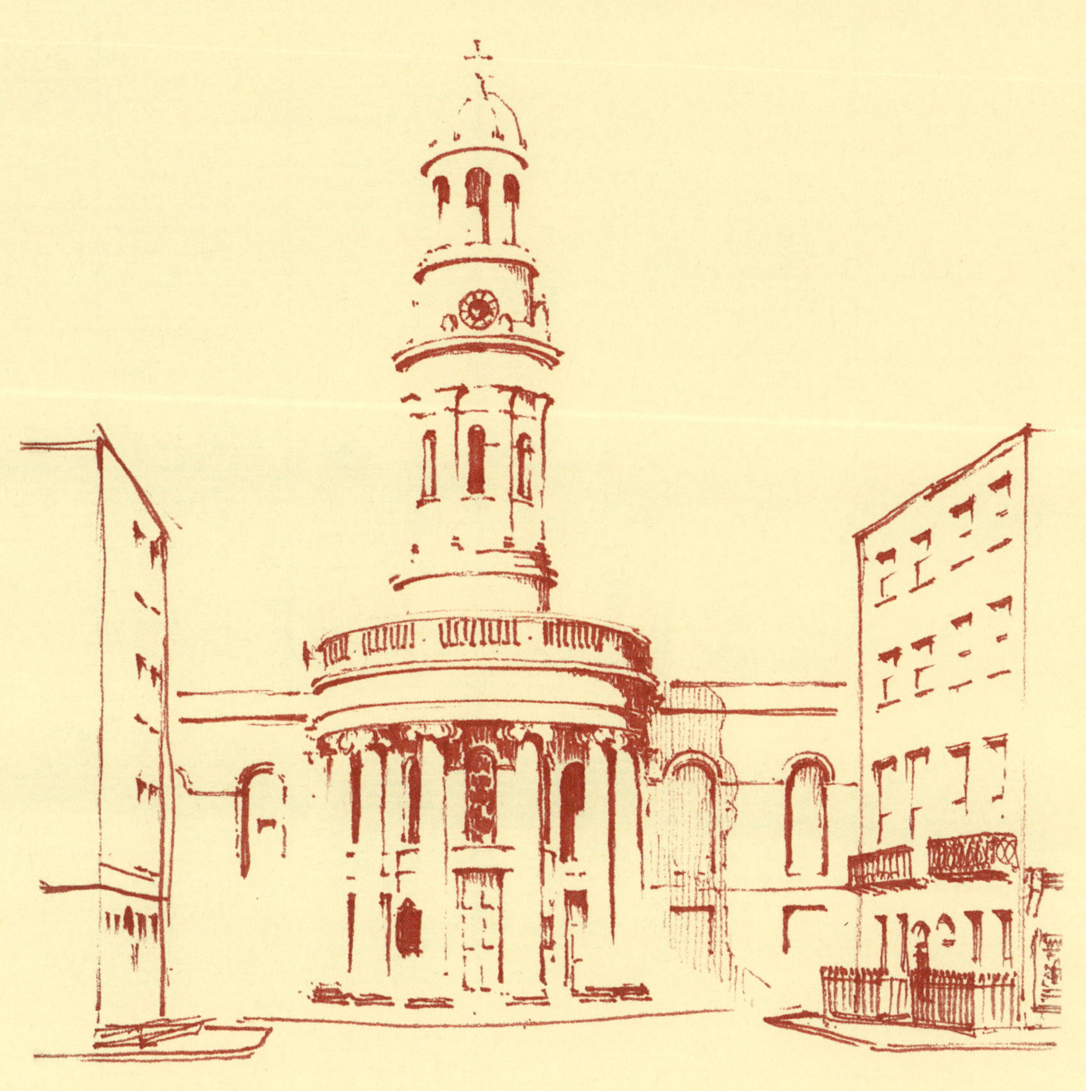

ST. MARY, WYNDHAM PLACE BY SMIRKE A.C.66

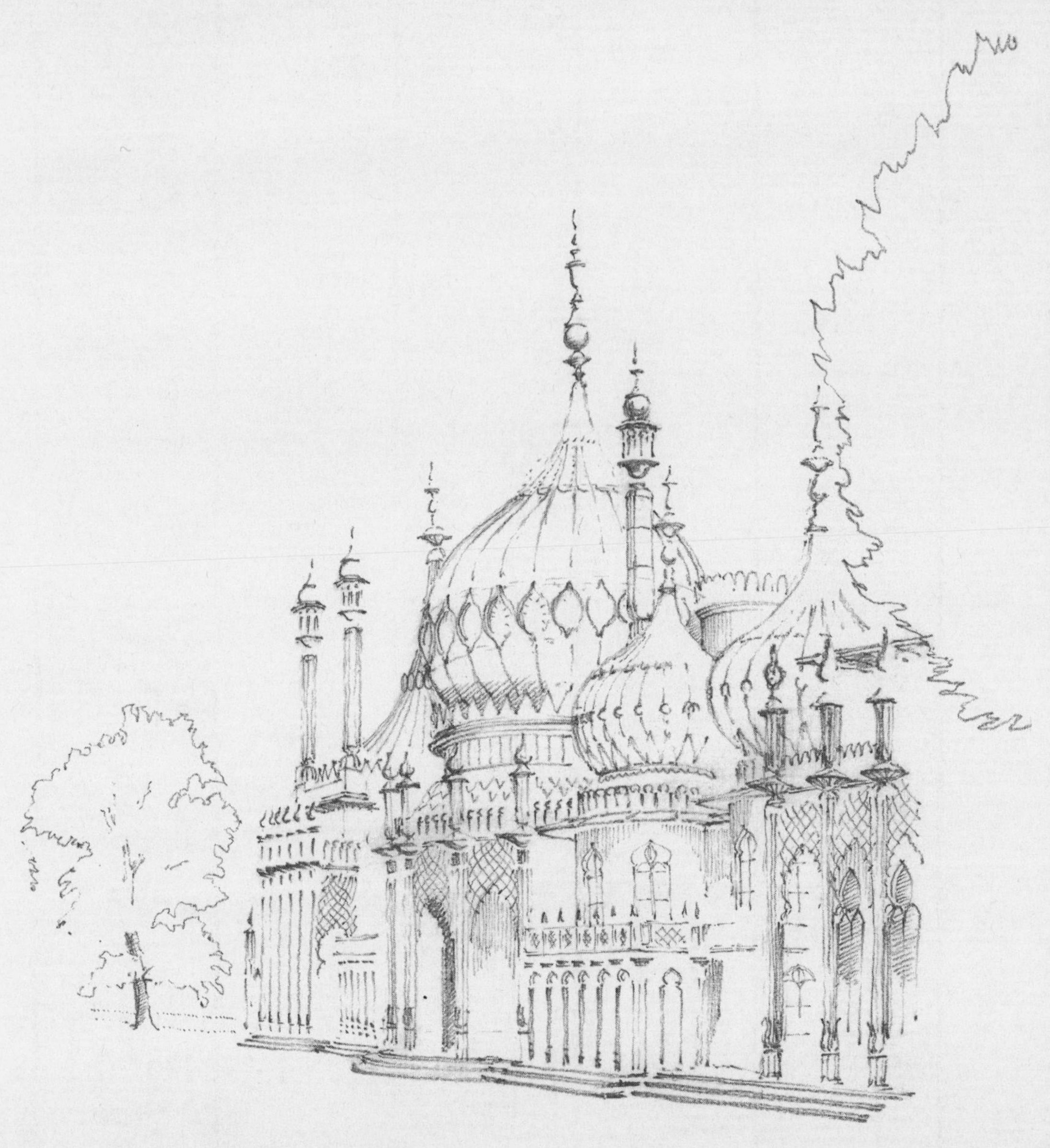

BRIGHTON PAVILION BY NASH A.C.77

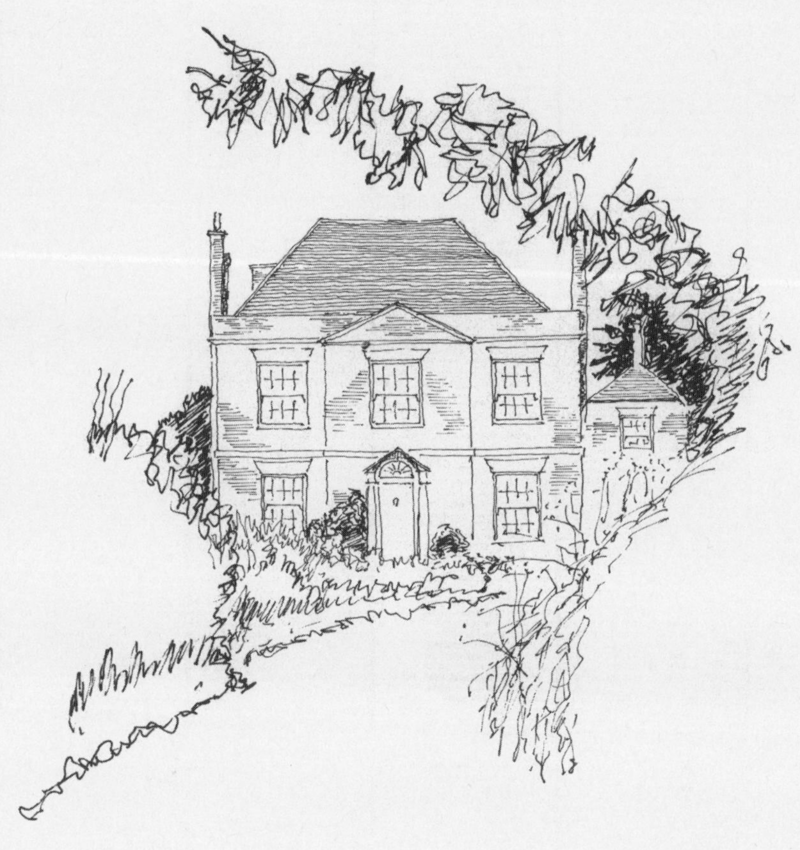

KENT HOUSE, S. HARTING

A.C. 76

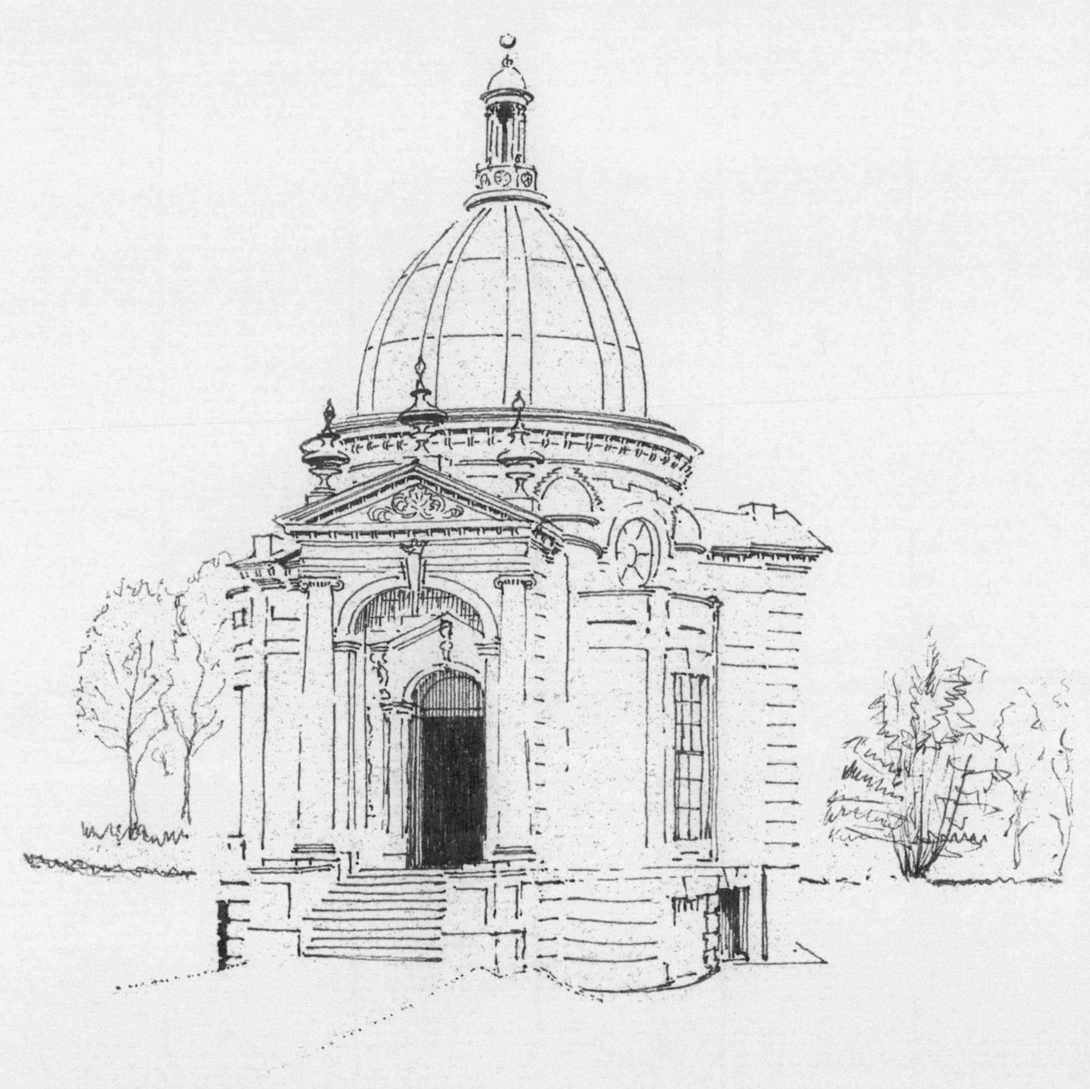

WREST PARK PAVILION BY ARCHER A.C. 78

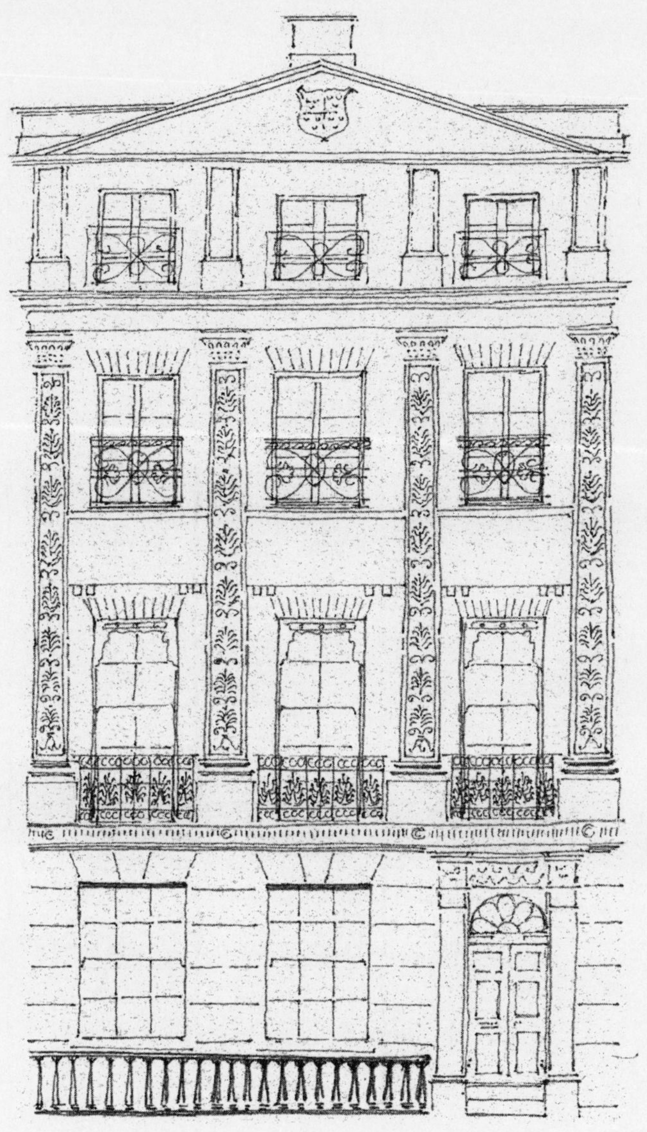

ADELPHI REMNANT BY ADAM A.C. 76

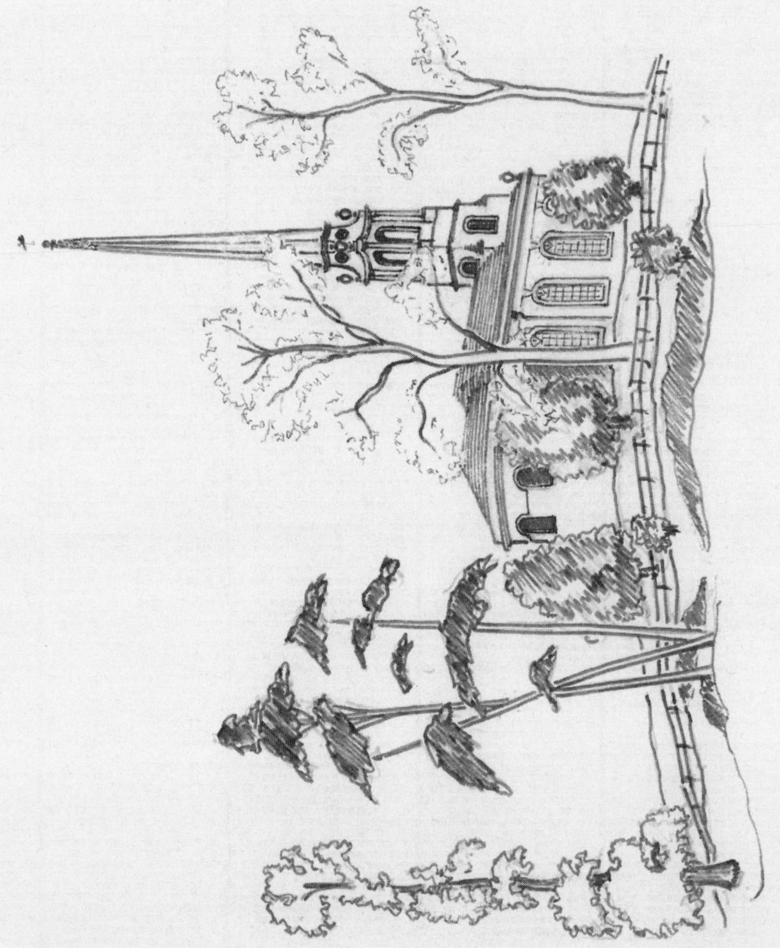

TARDEBIGGE BY FRANCIS HIORNE

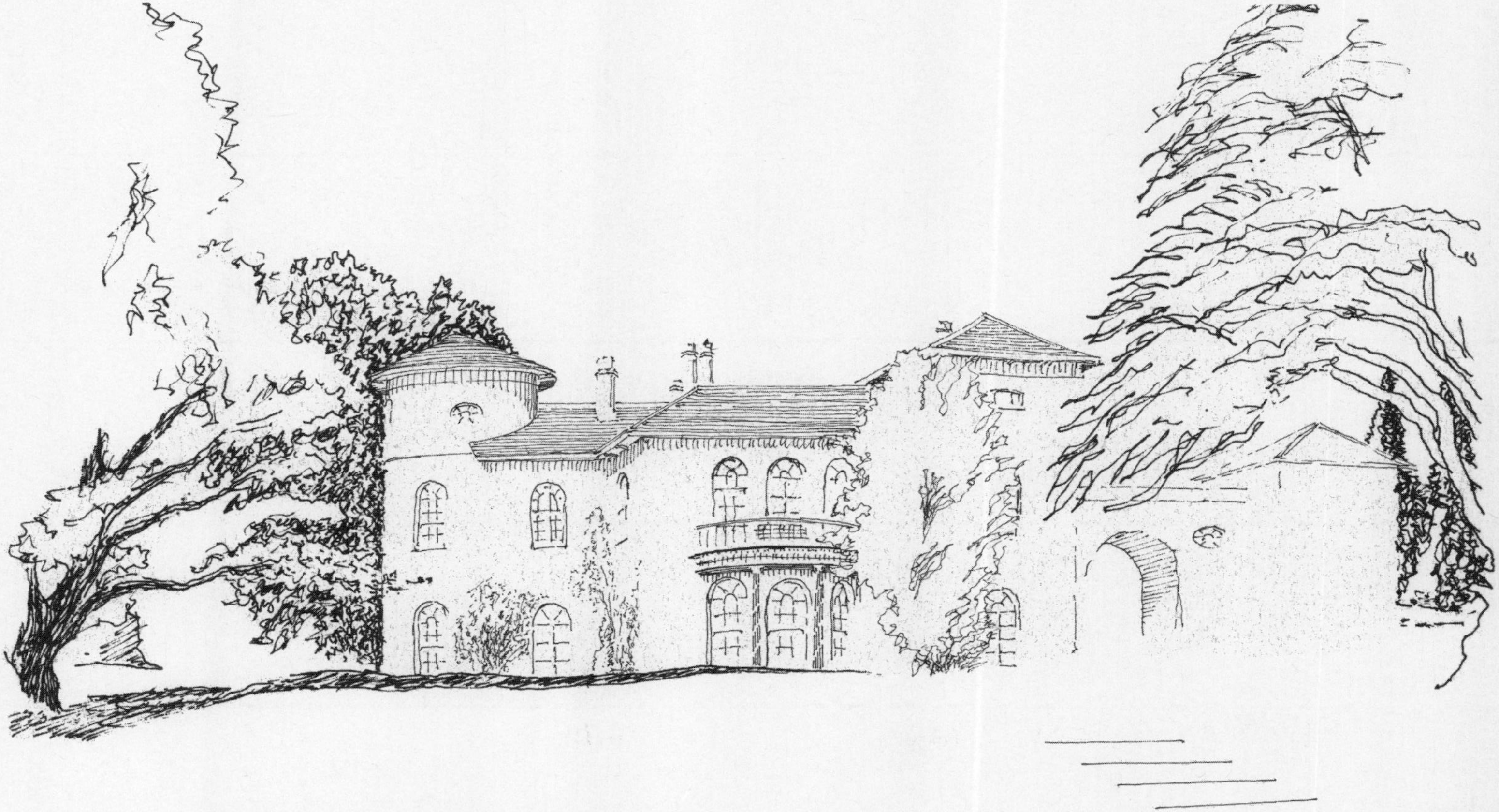

SANDRIDGE, DEVON BY NASH

A.C. 76

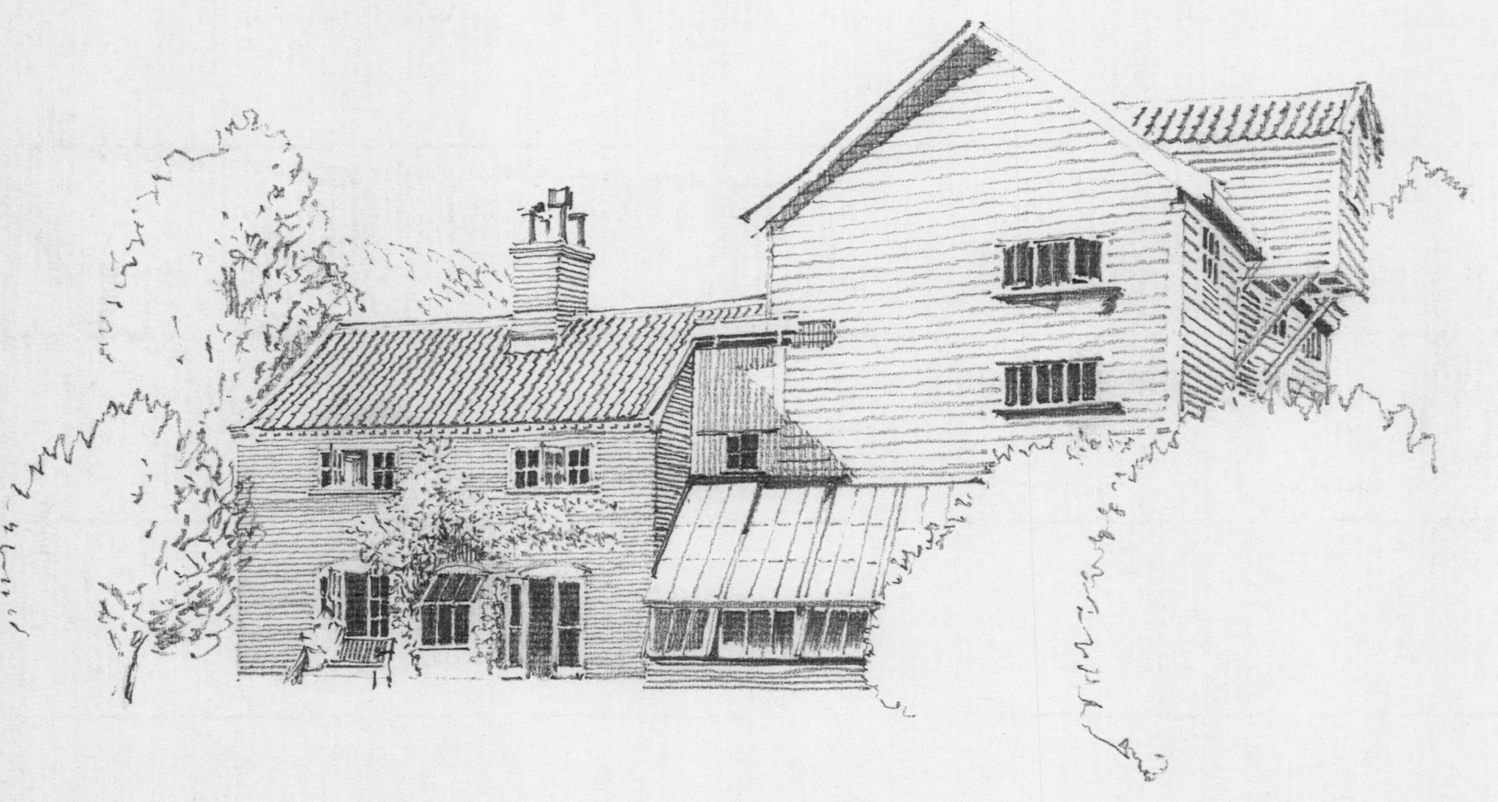

FRIDA & VICS' MILL.

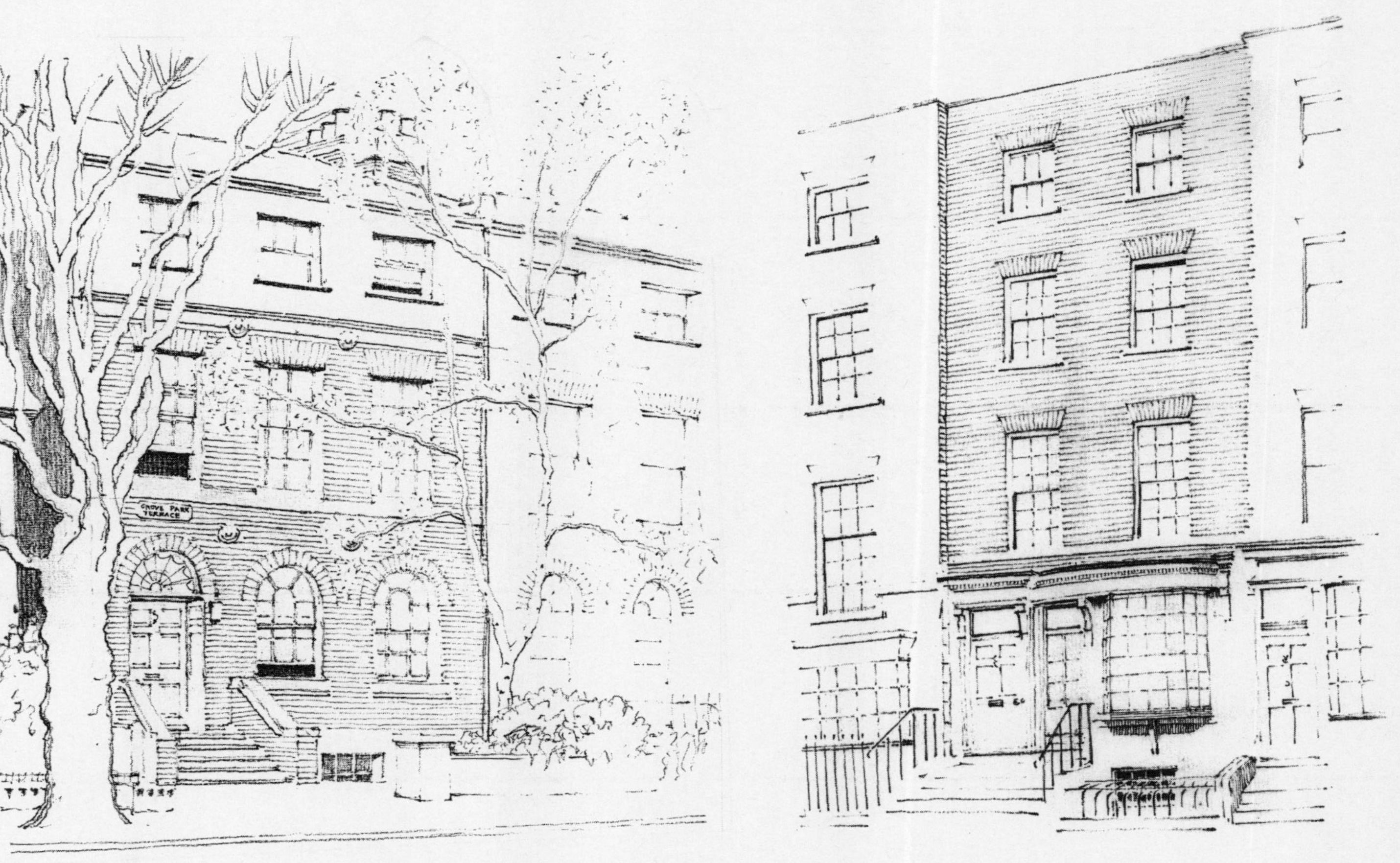

JENNINGS' HOUSE A C 88

WILLOW'S HOUSE A.C. 90

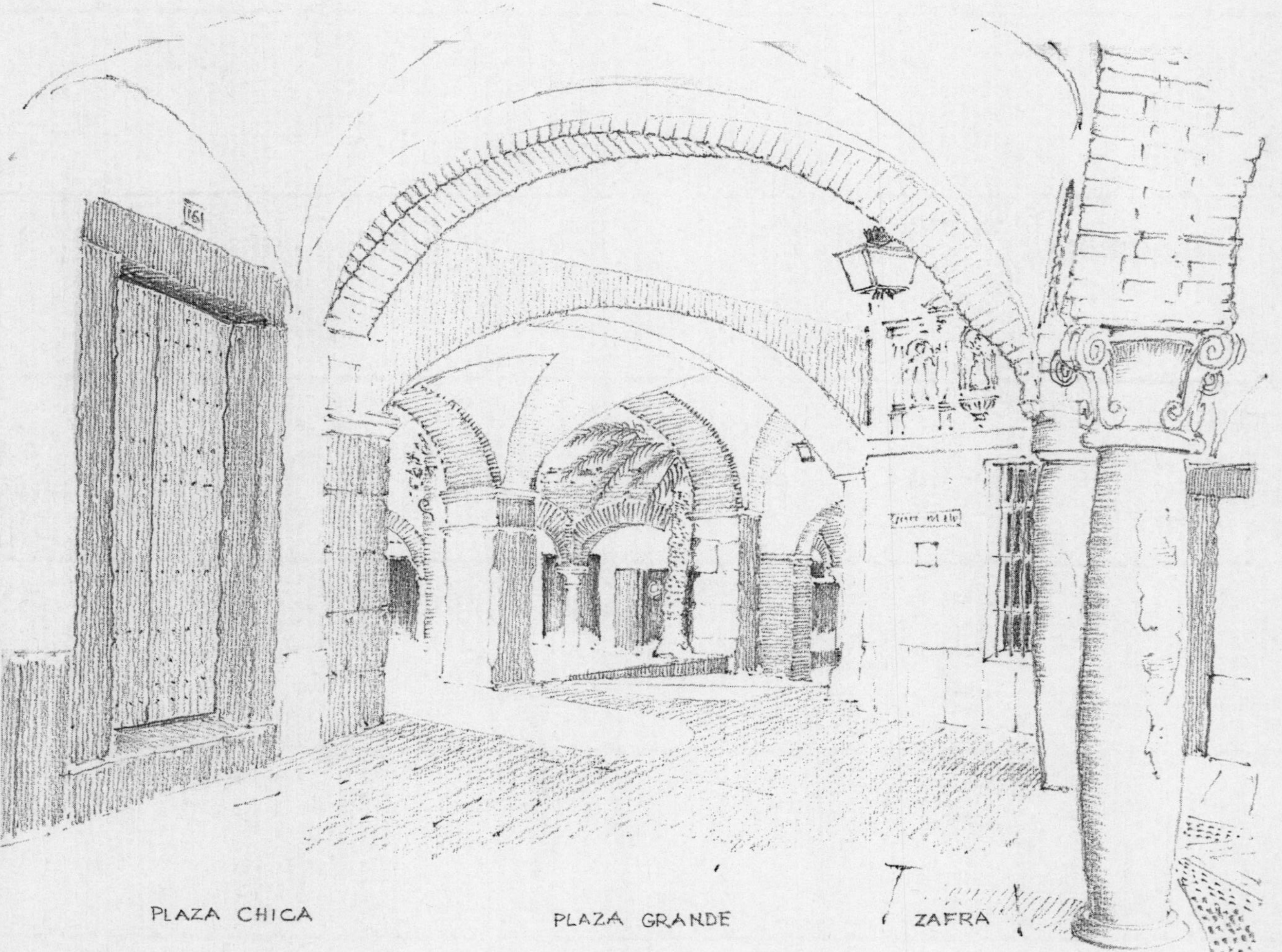

PLAZA CHICA PLAZA GRANDE ZAFRA

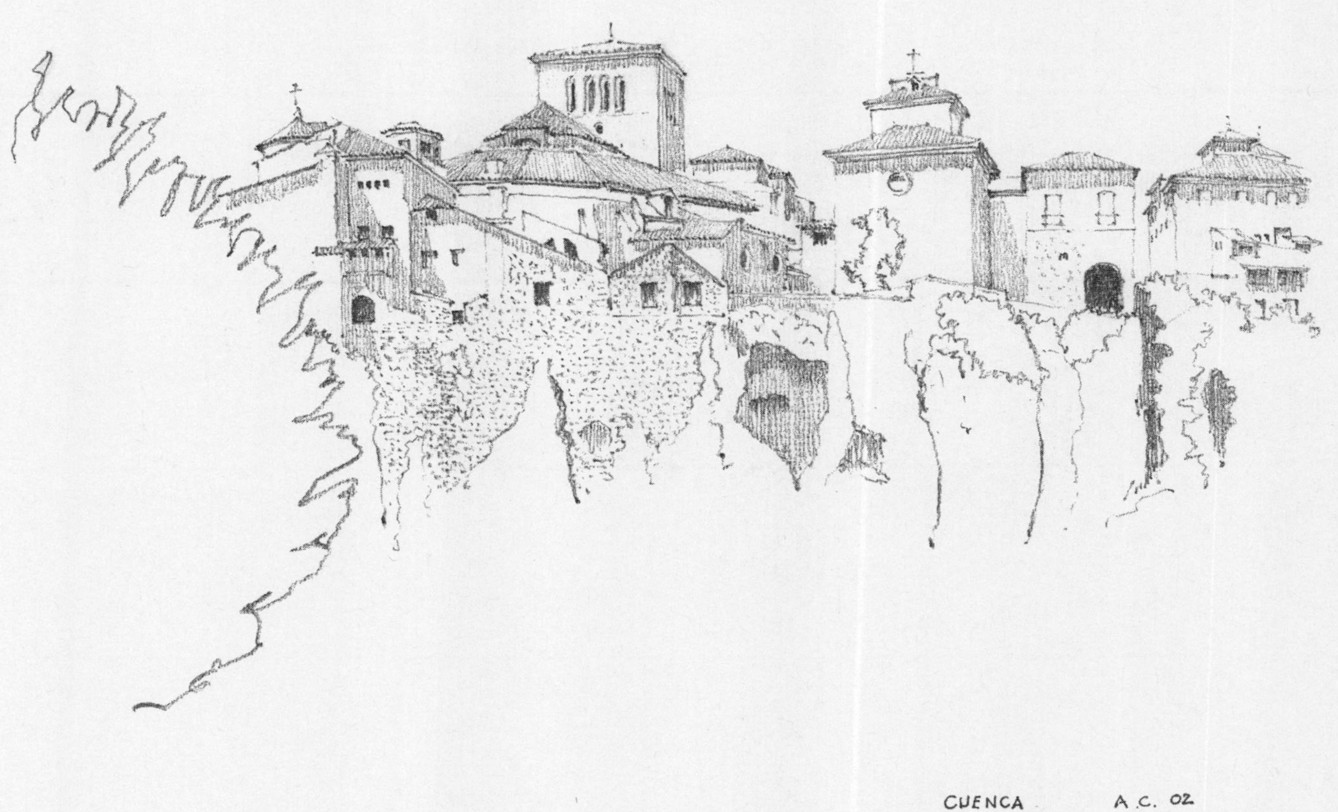
CUENCA A.C. 02

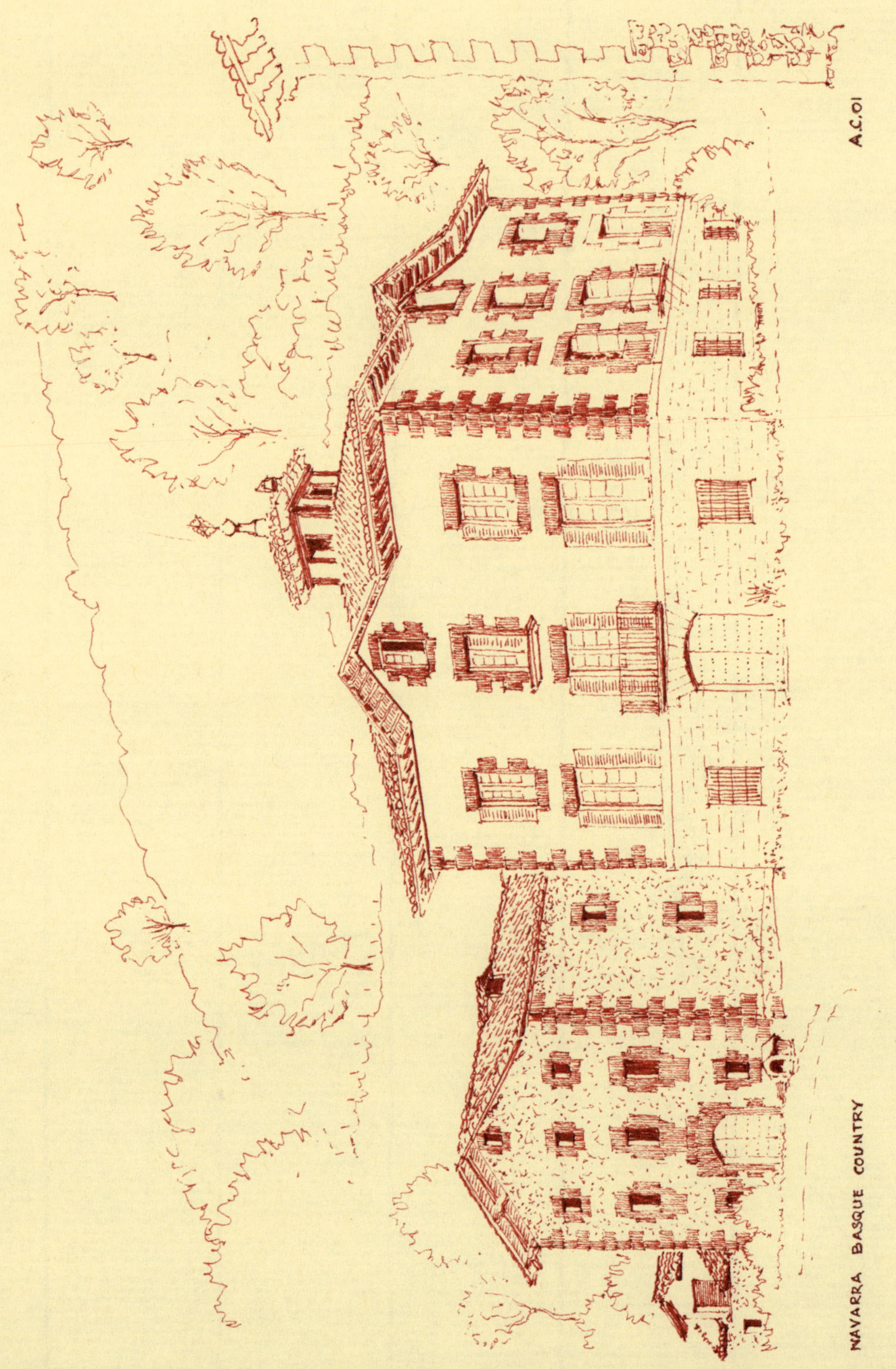

NAVARRA BASQUE COUNTRY

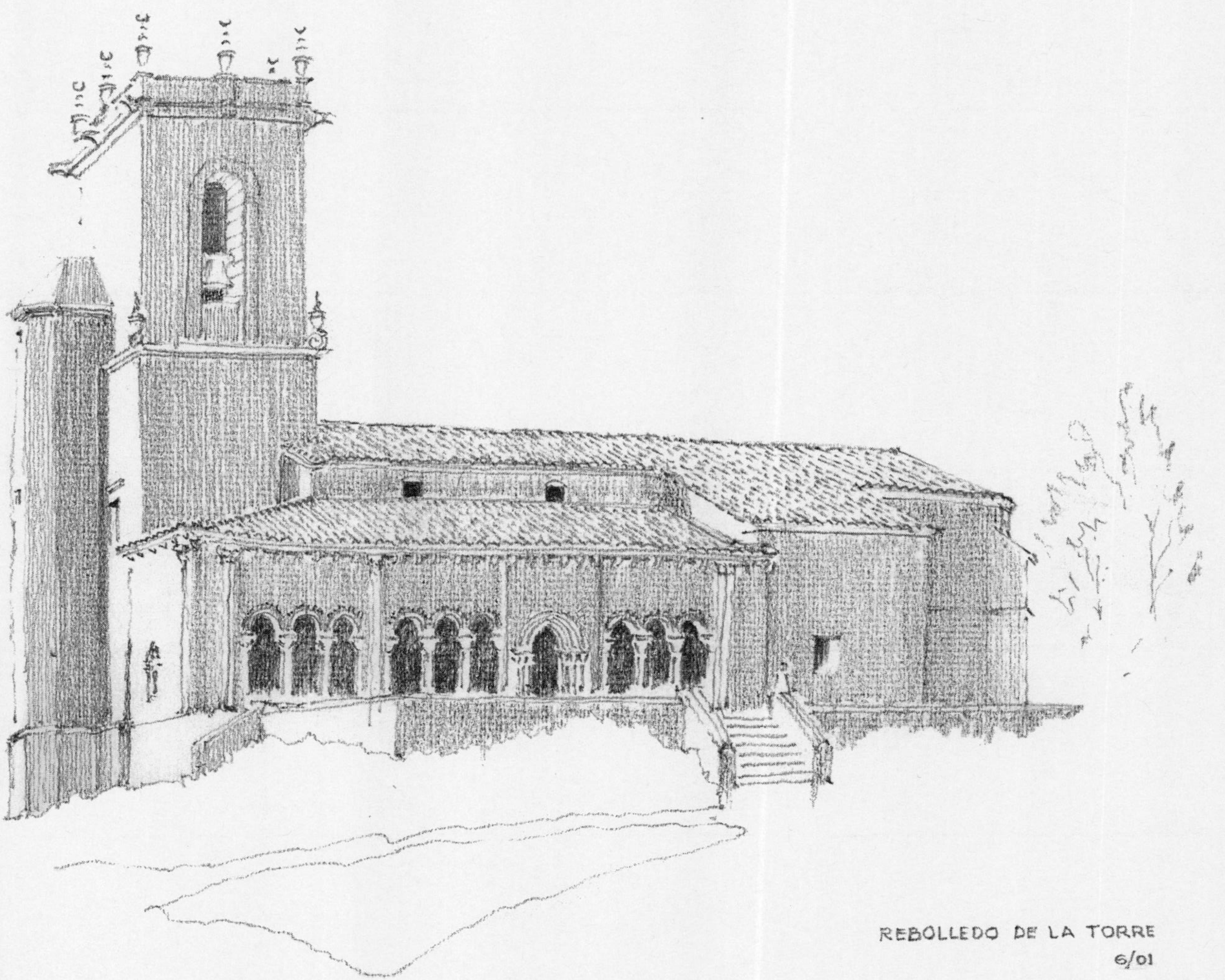
REBOLLEDO DE LA TORRE
6/01

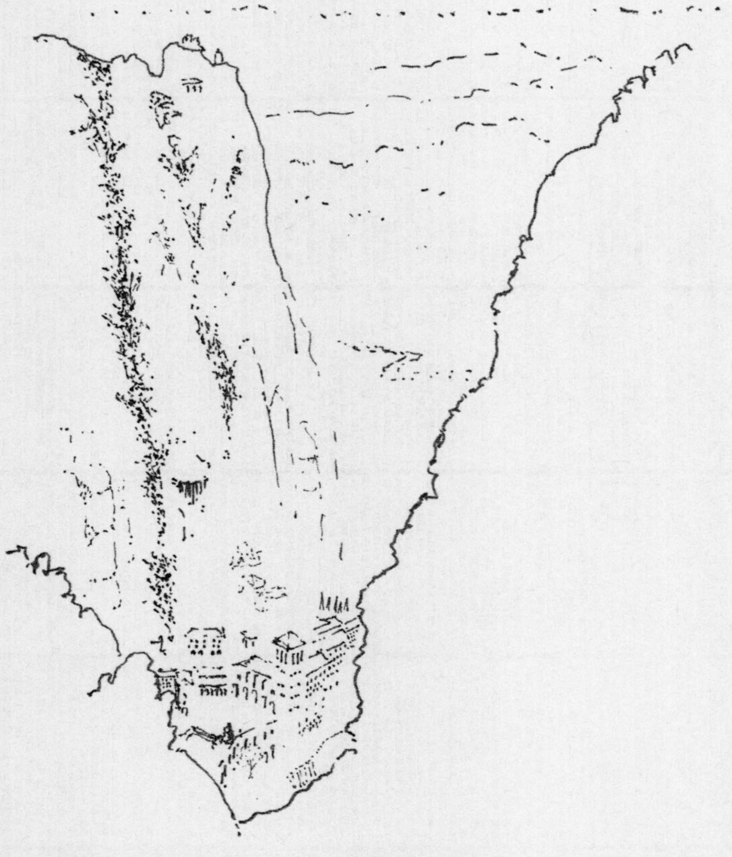

MONTSERRAT MONASTERY AC 75

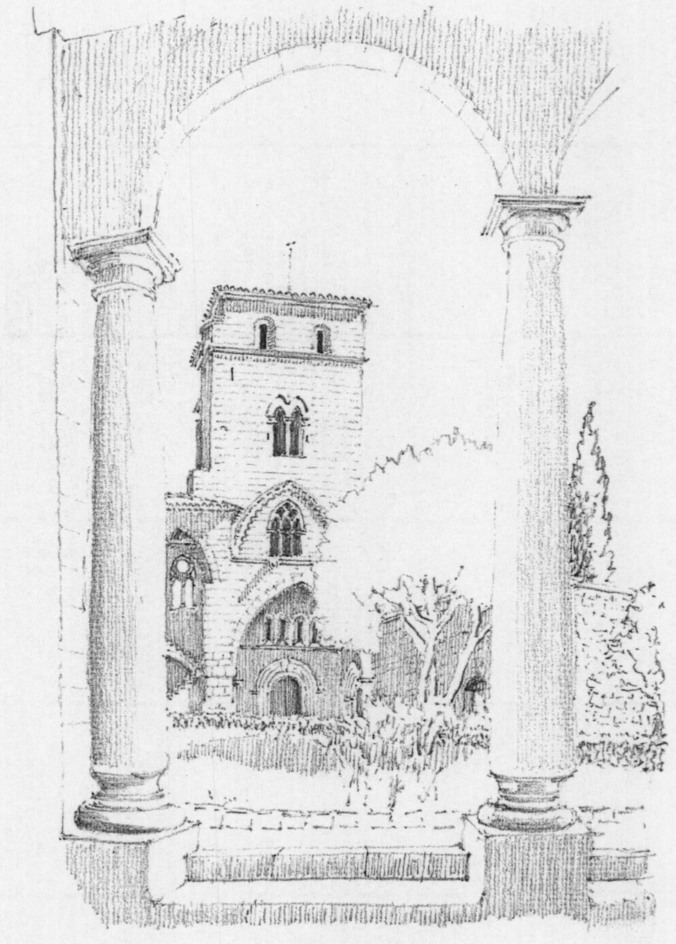

ALCAÑIZ AC 02

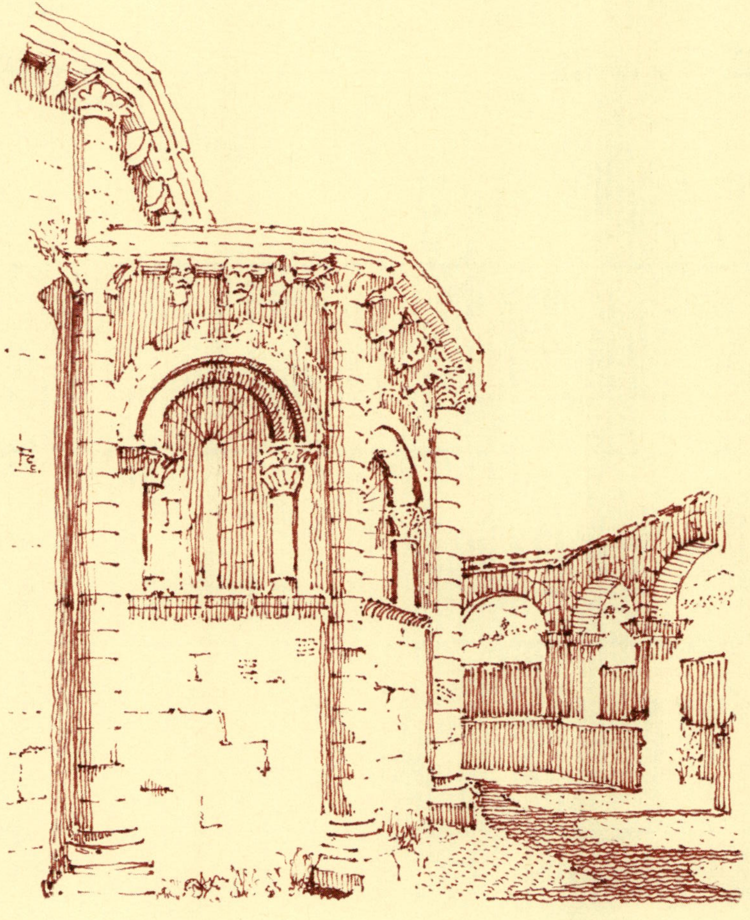

EUENATE A.G. 86

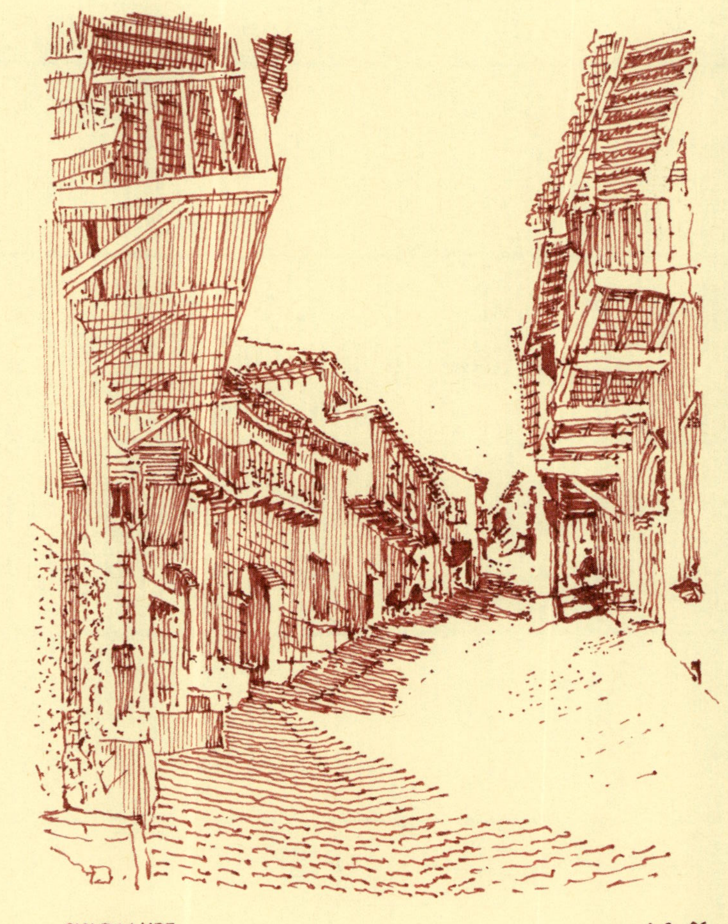

GUADALUPE A.G 86

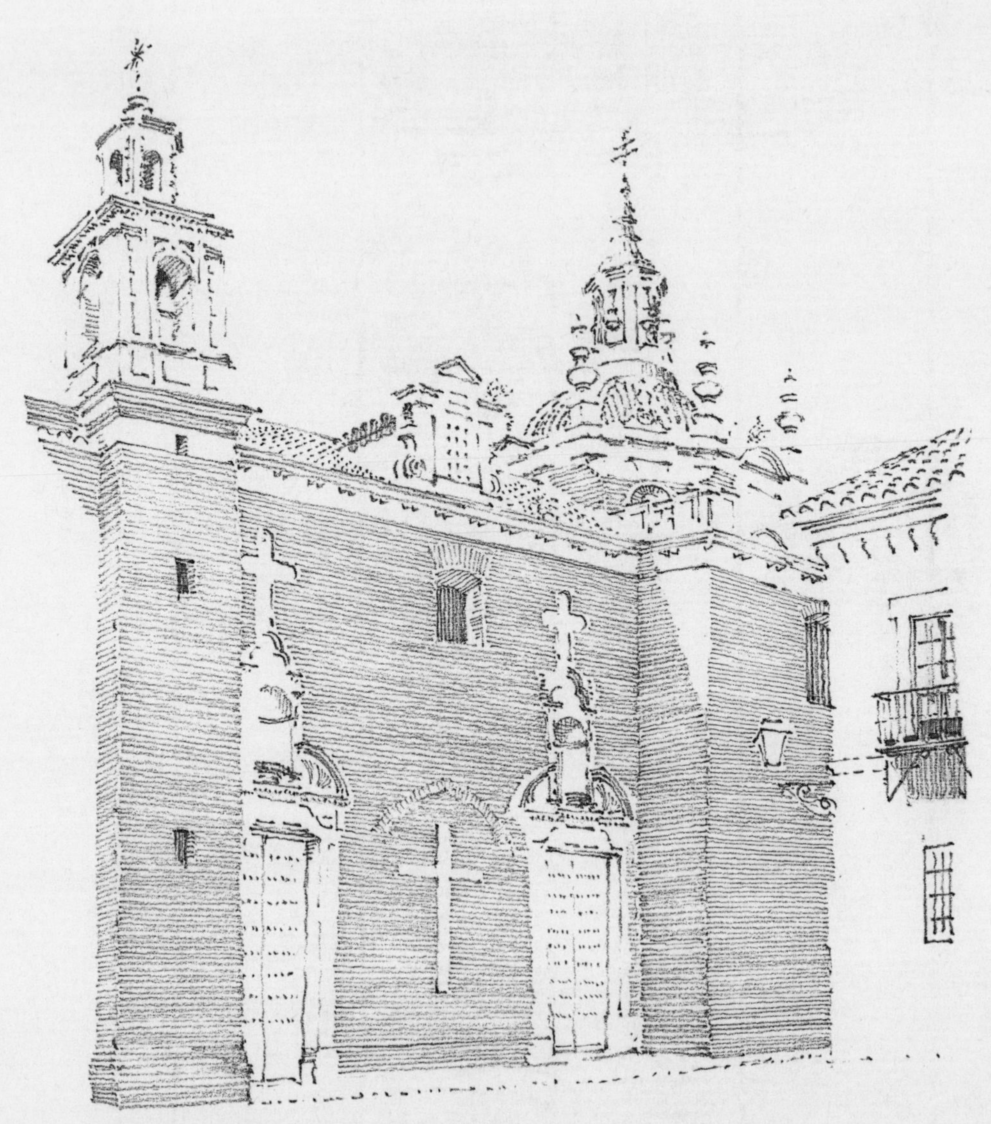

CARMONA A.C. 89

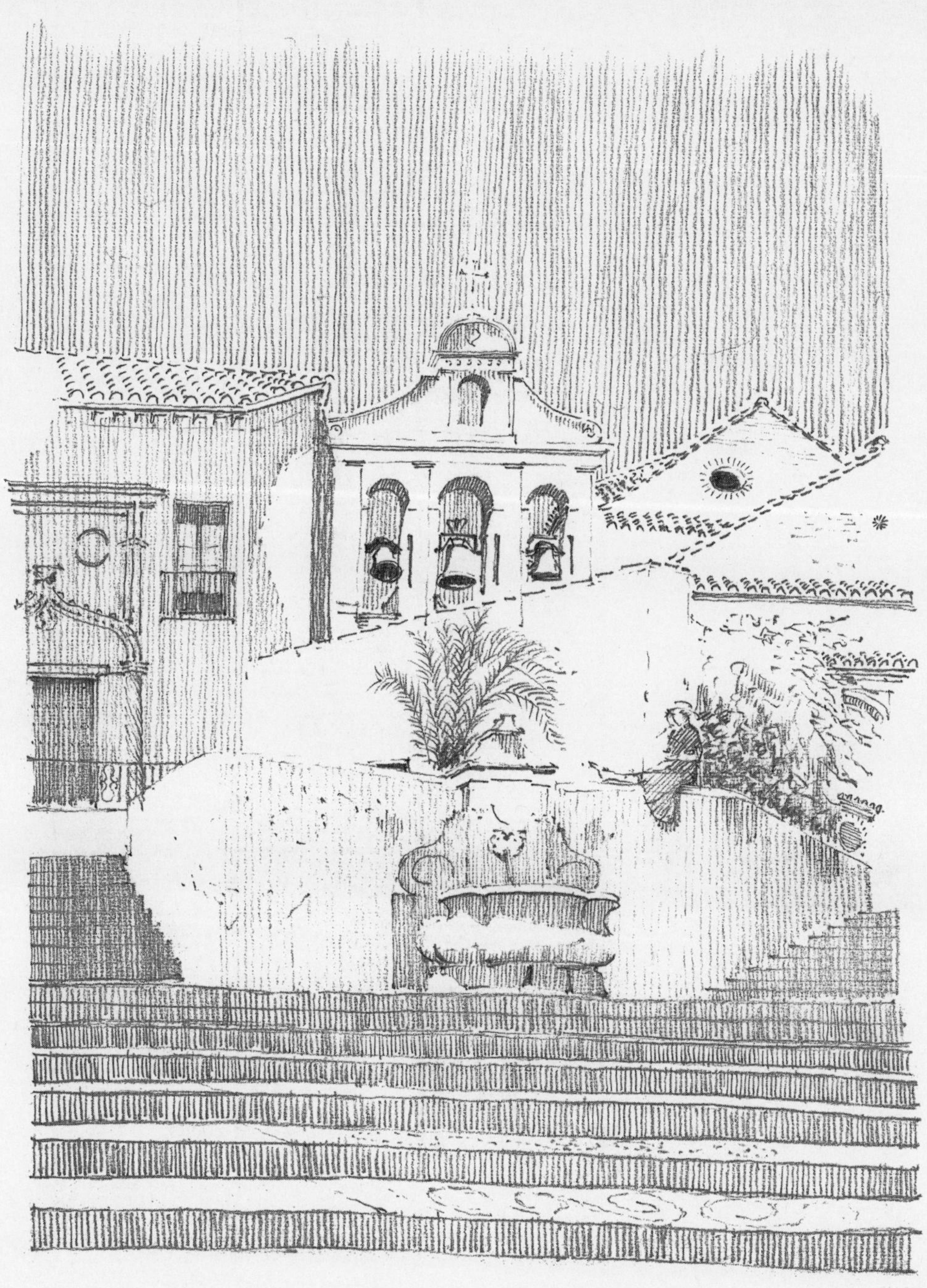

CORDOBA A.C. 89

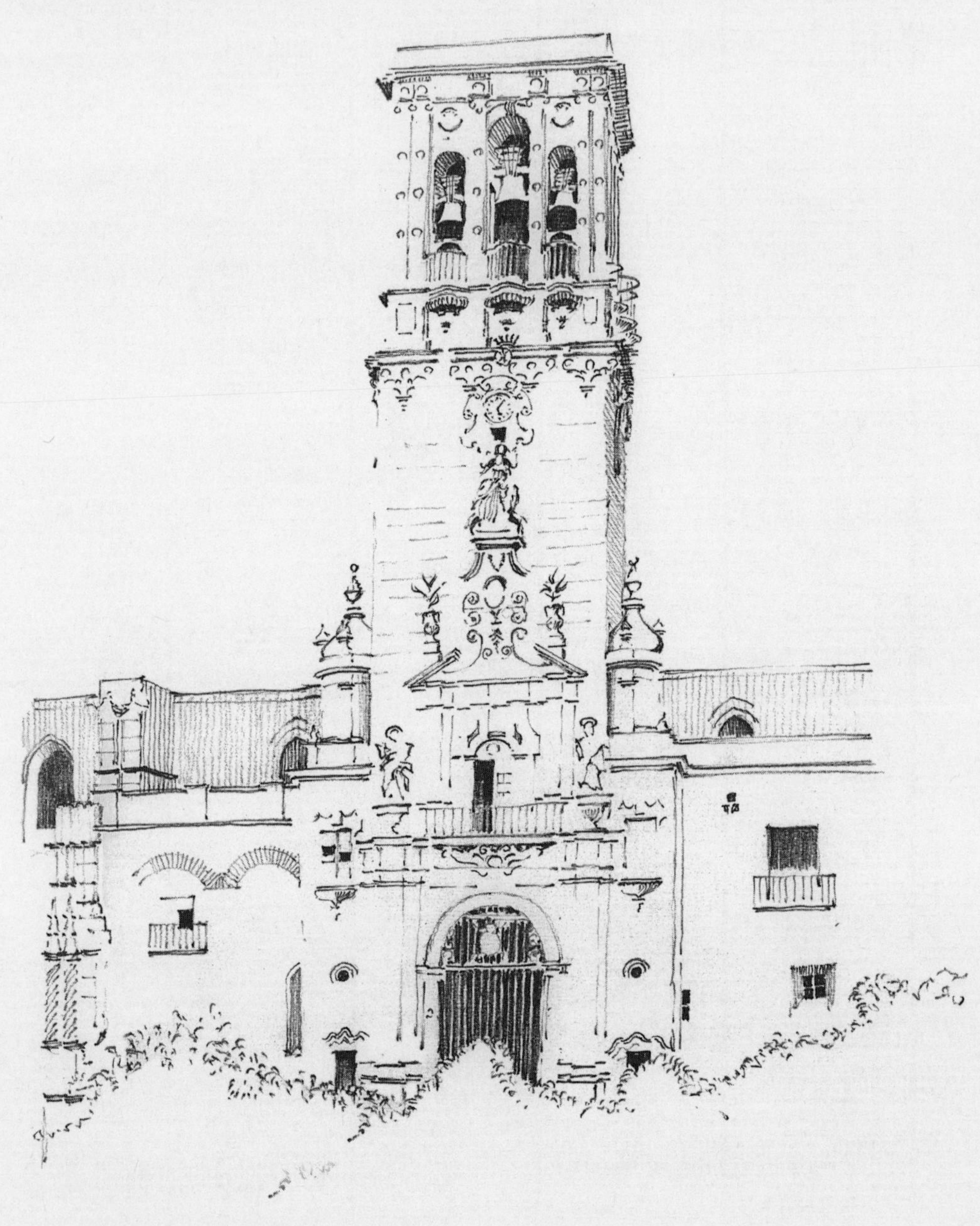

ARCOS CATHEDRAL A.C. 89

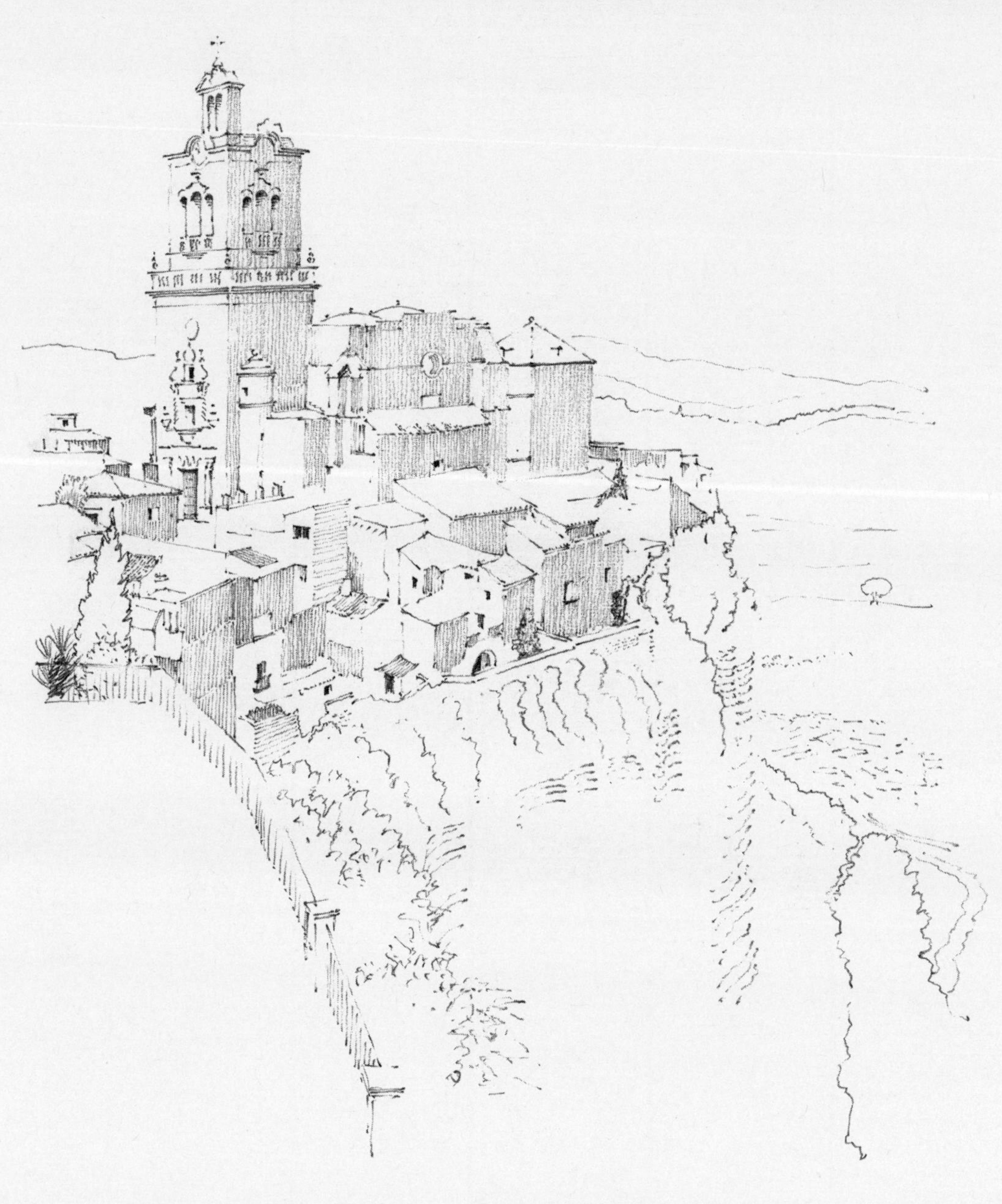

ARCOS DELLA FRONTERA   A C 89

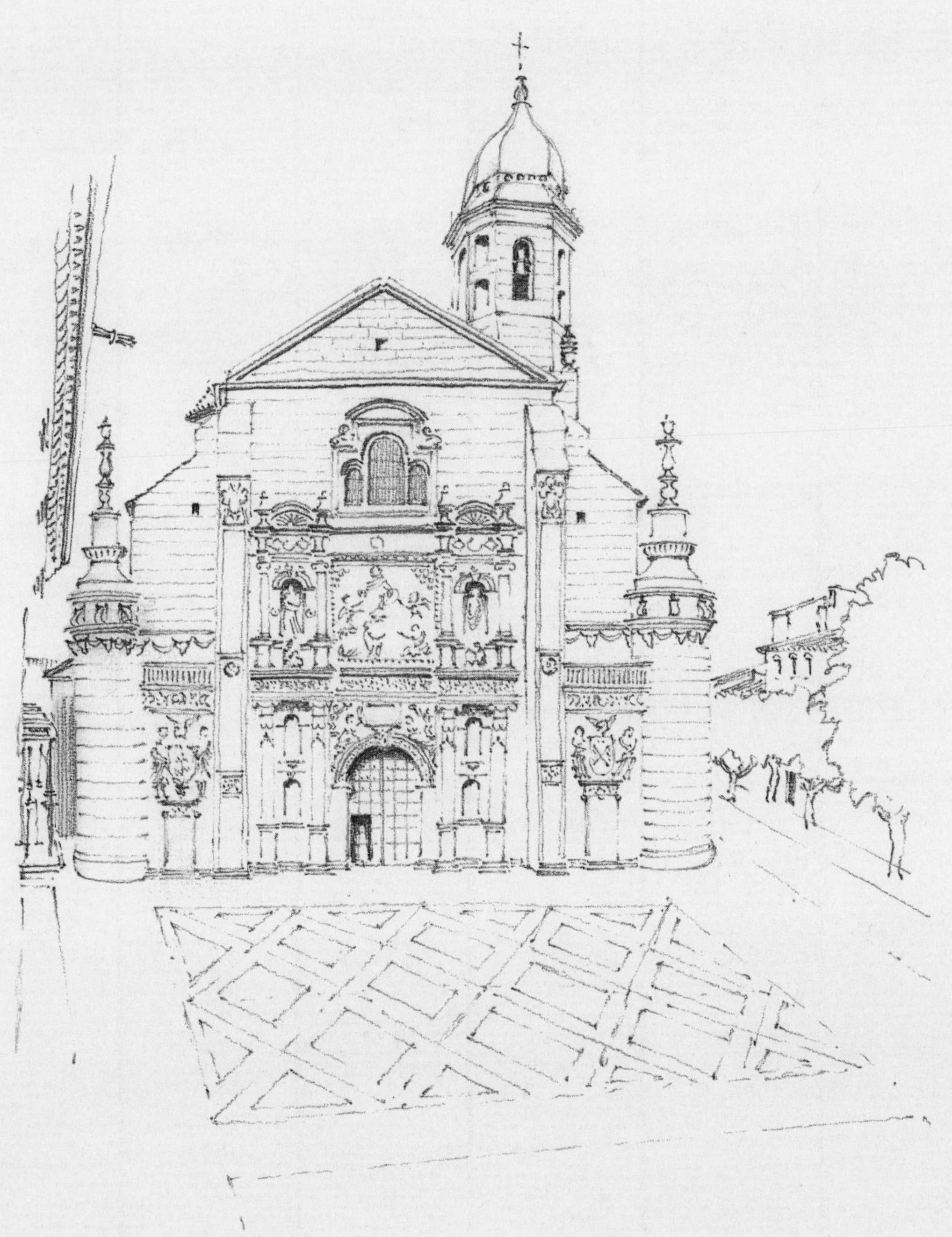

SACRA CAPILLA DEL SALVADOR, UBEDA

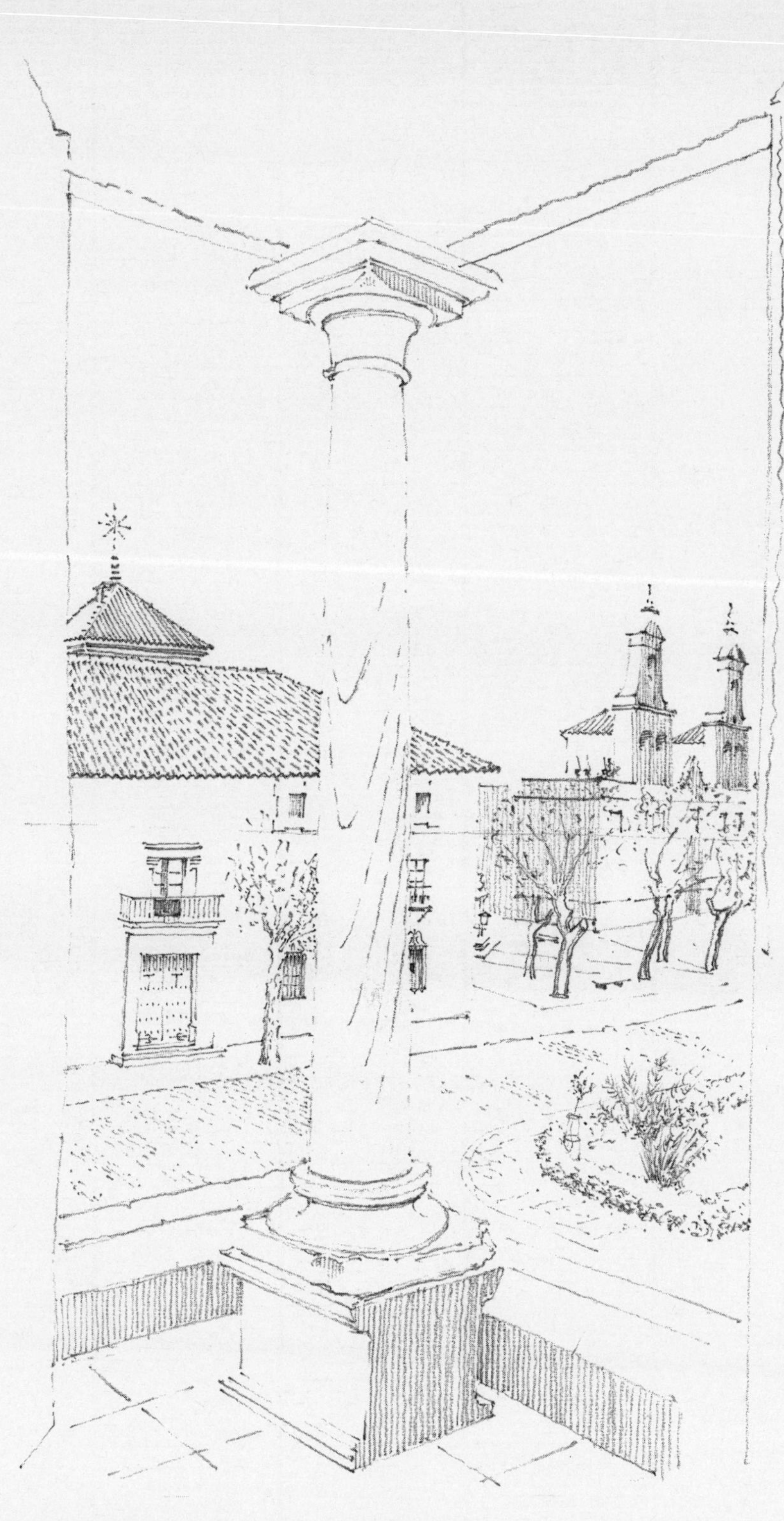

PARADOR, UBEDA A.C. 89

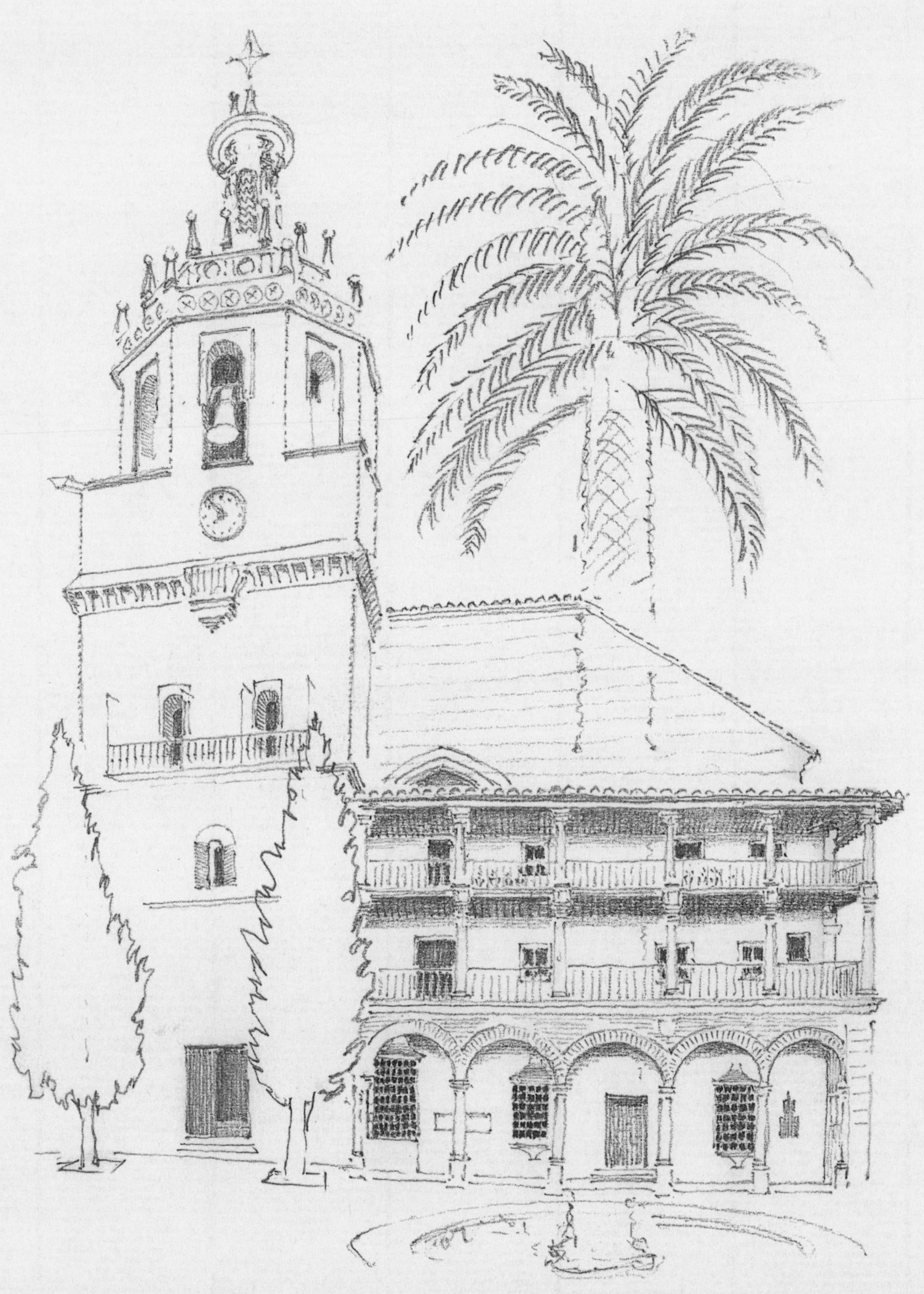

RONDA CATHEDRAL A.C. 02

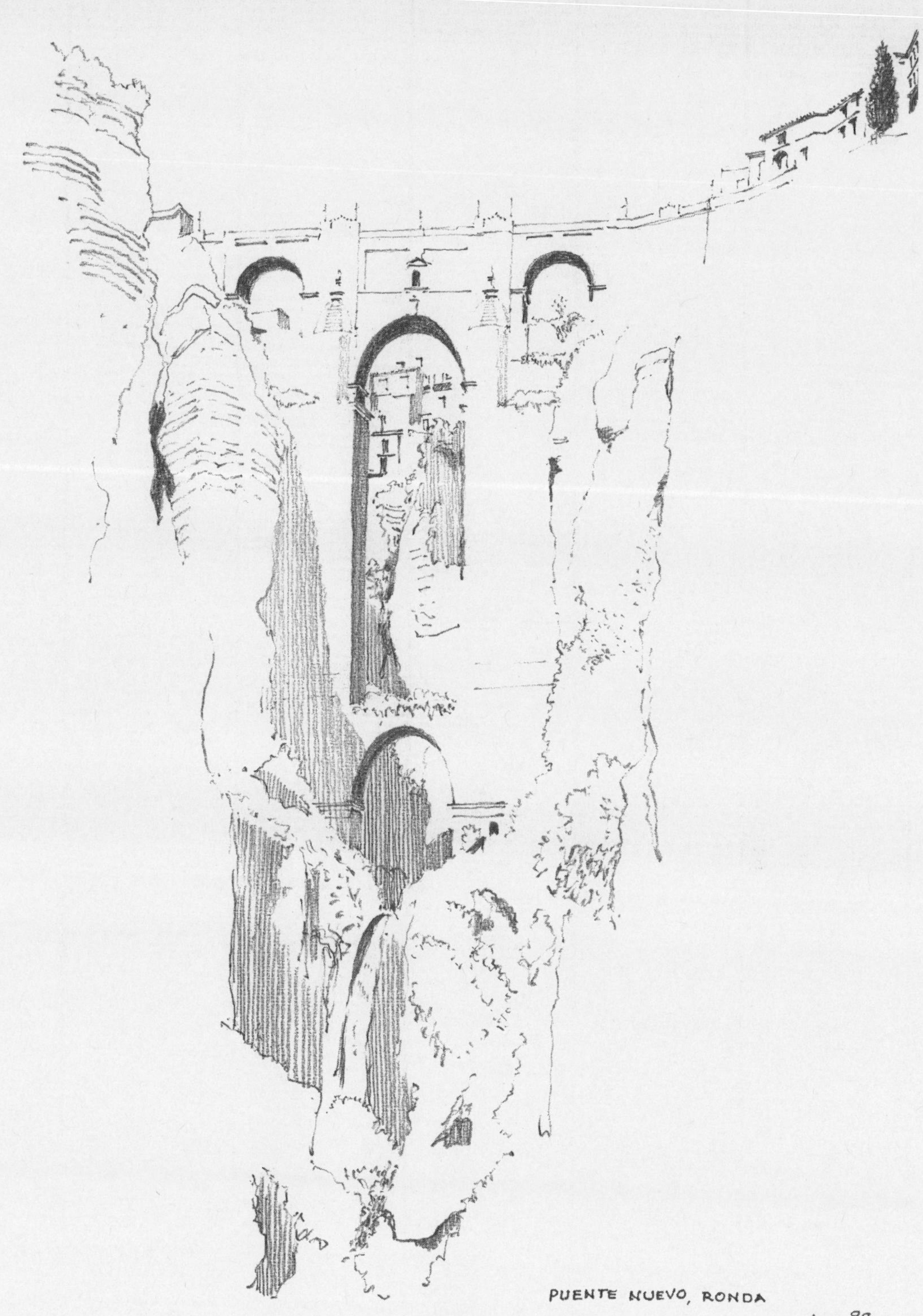
PUENTE NUEVO, RONDA
A.C. 89

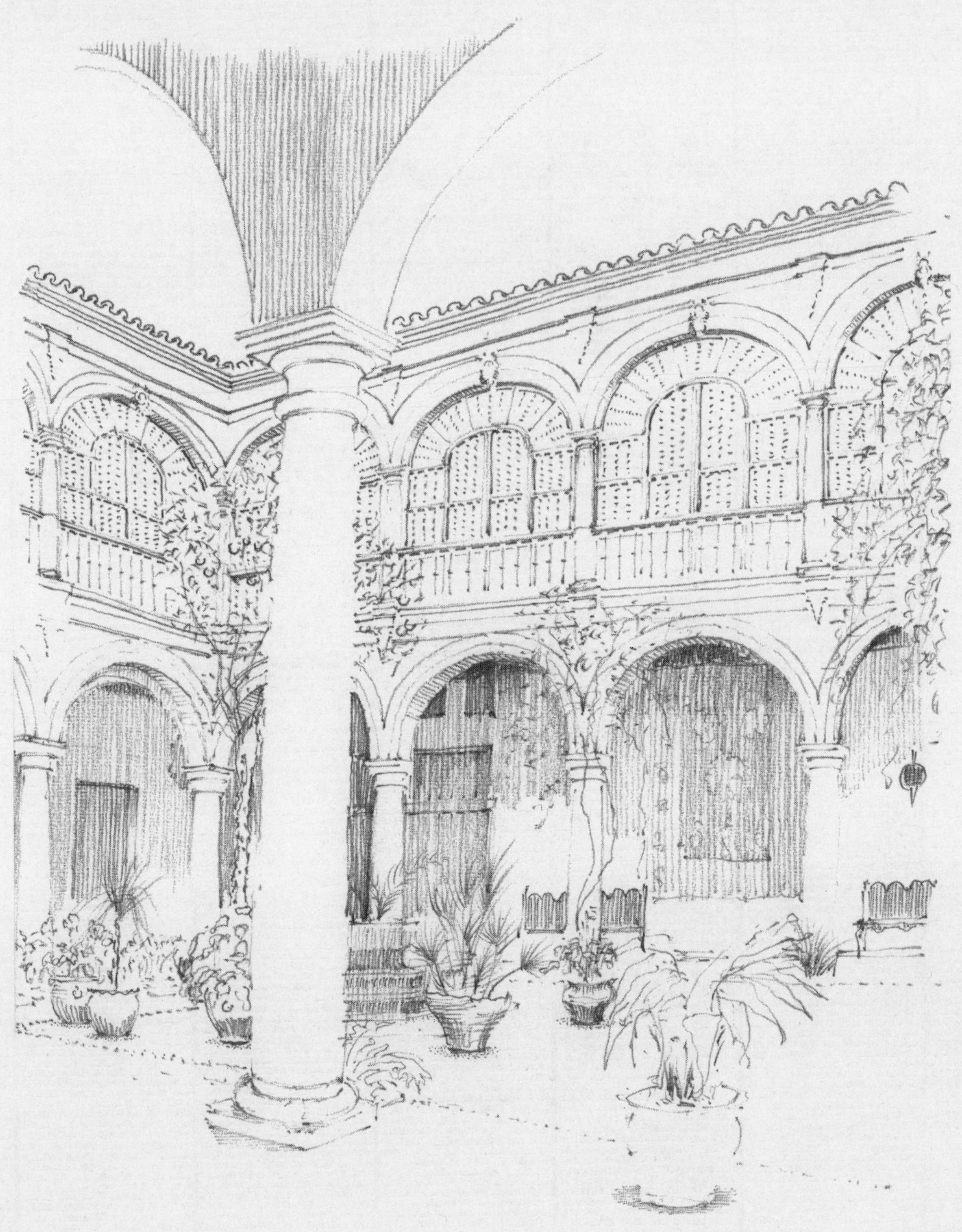

PARADOR, GRANADA AC 89

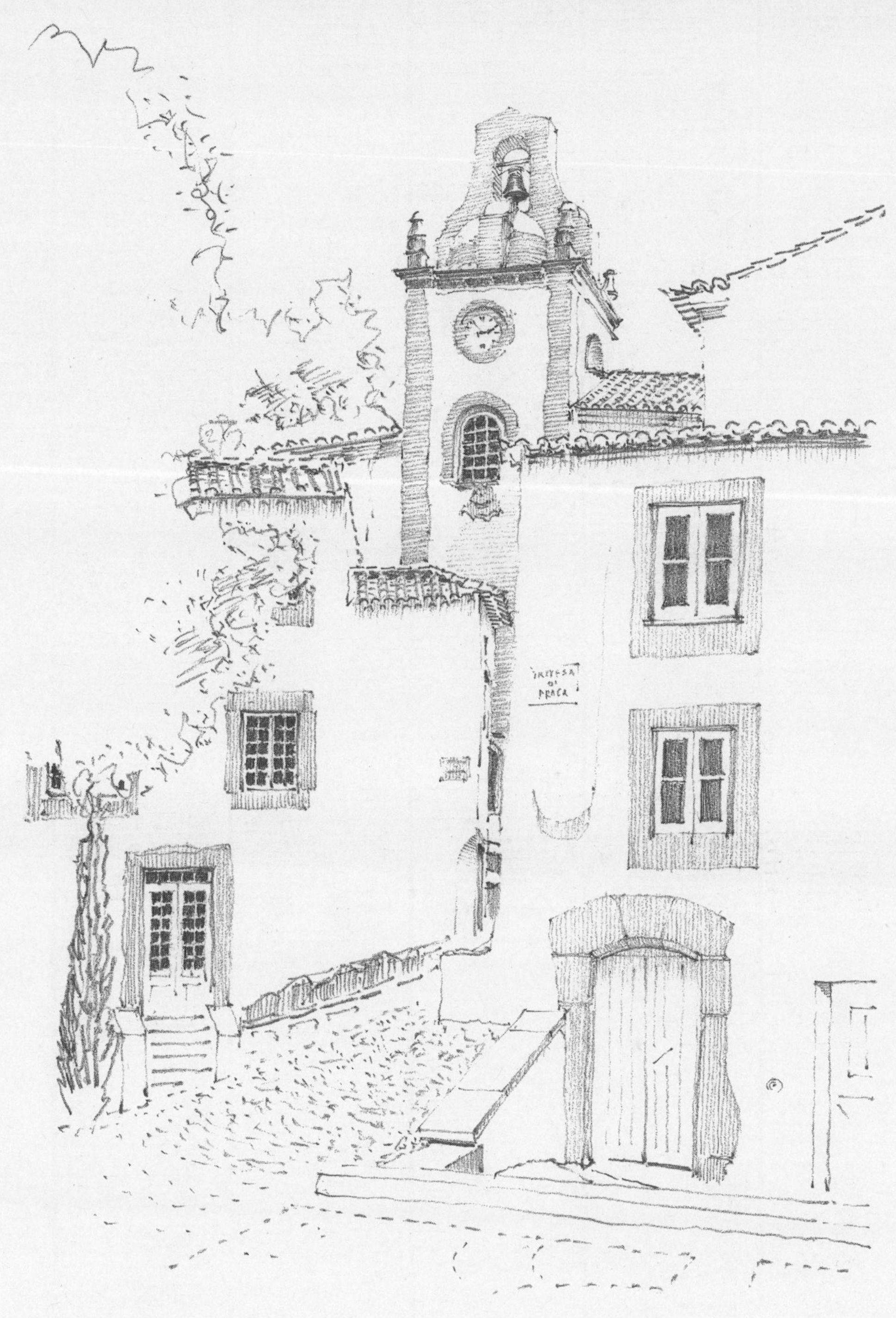

MARVAO, PORTUGAL AC 87

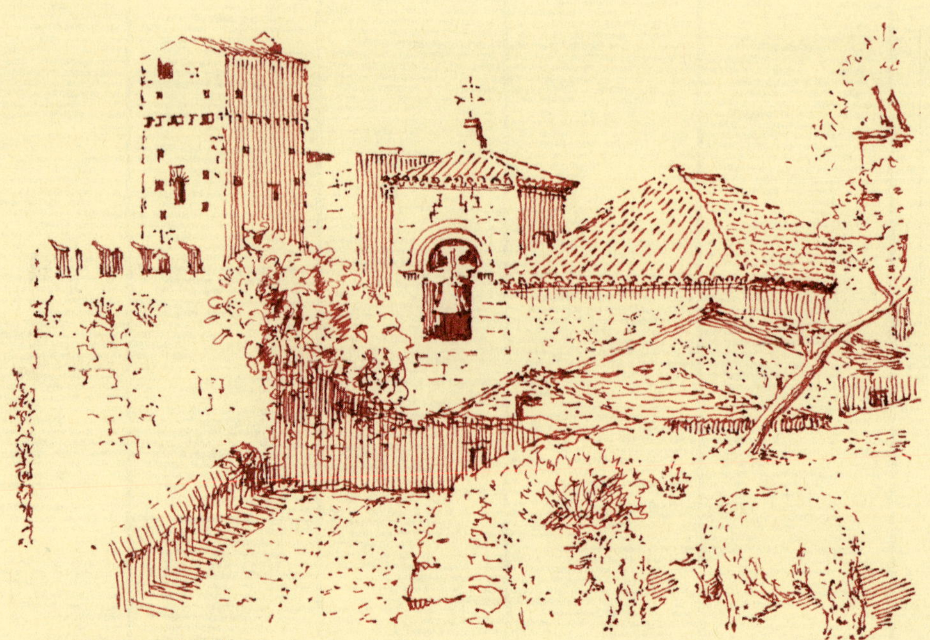

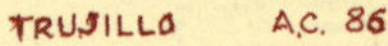

TRUJILLO A.C. 86

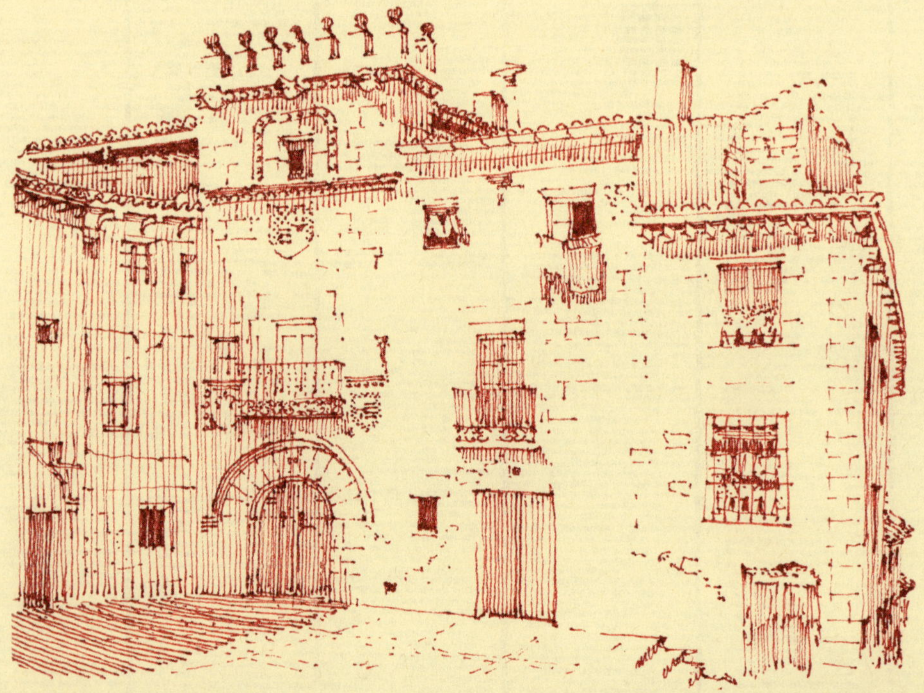

SIGUENZA, DONSEL'S HOUSE A C 86

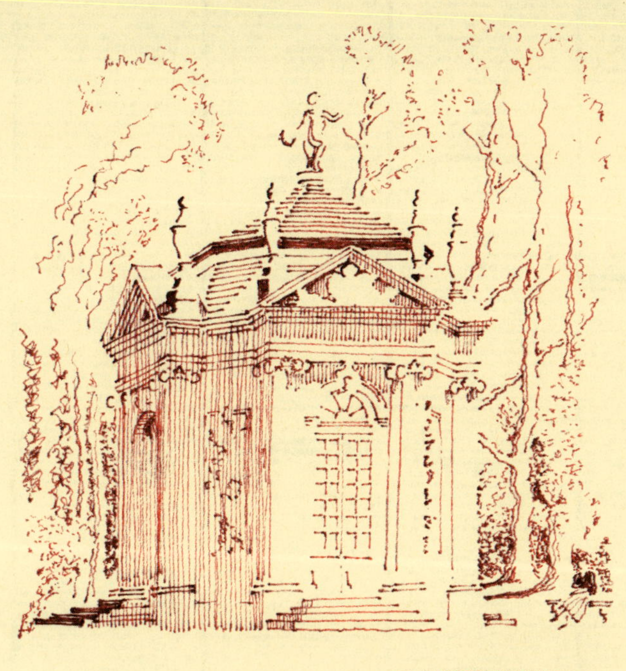

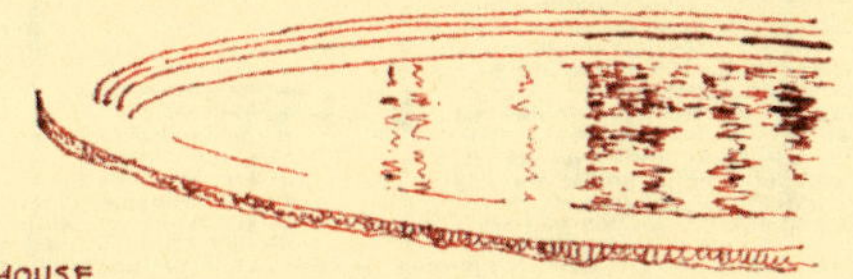

LA GRANJA, PUMP HOUSE

A.C 86

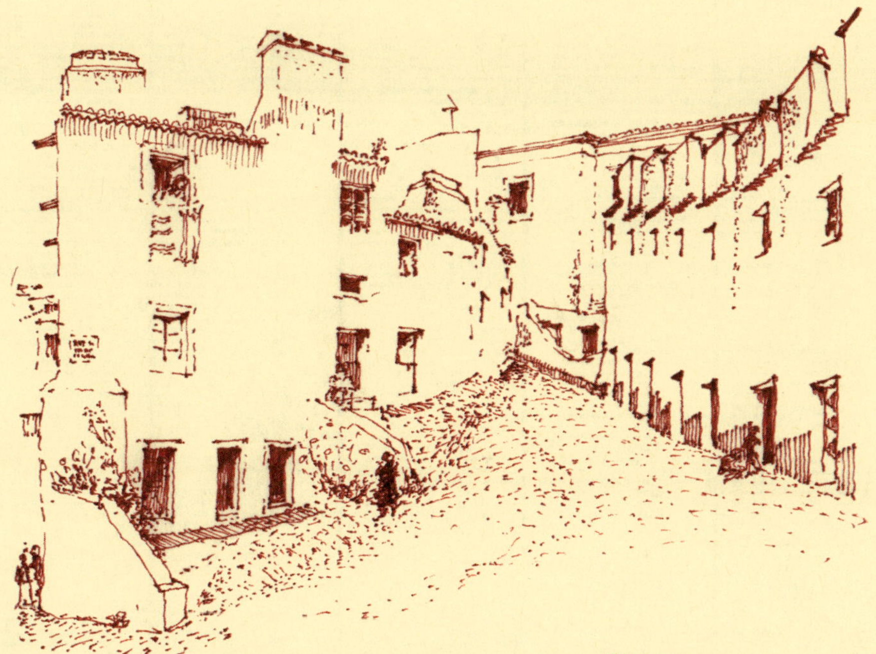

ELVAS PORTUGAL AC 87

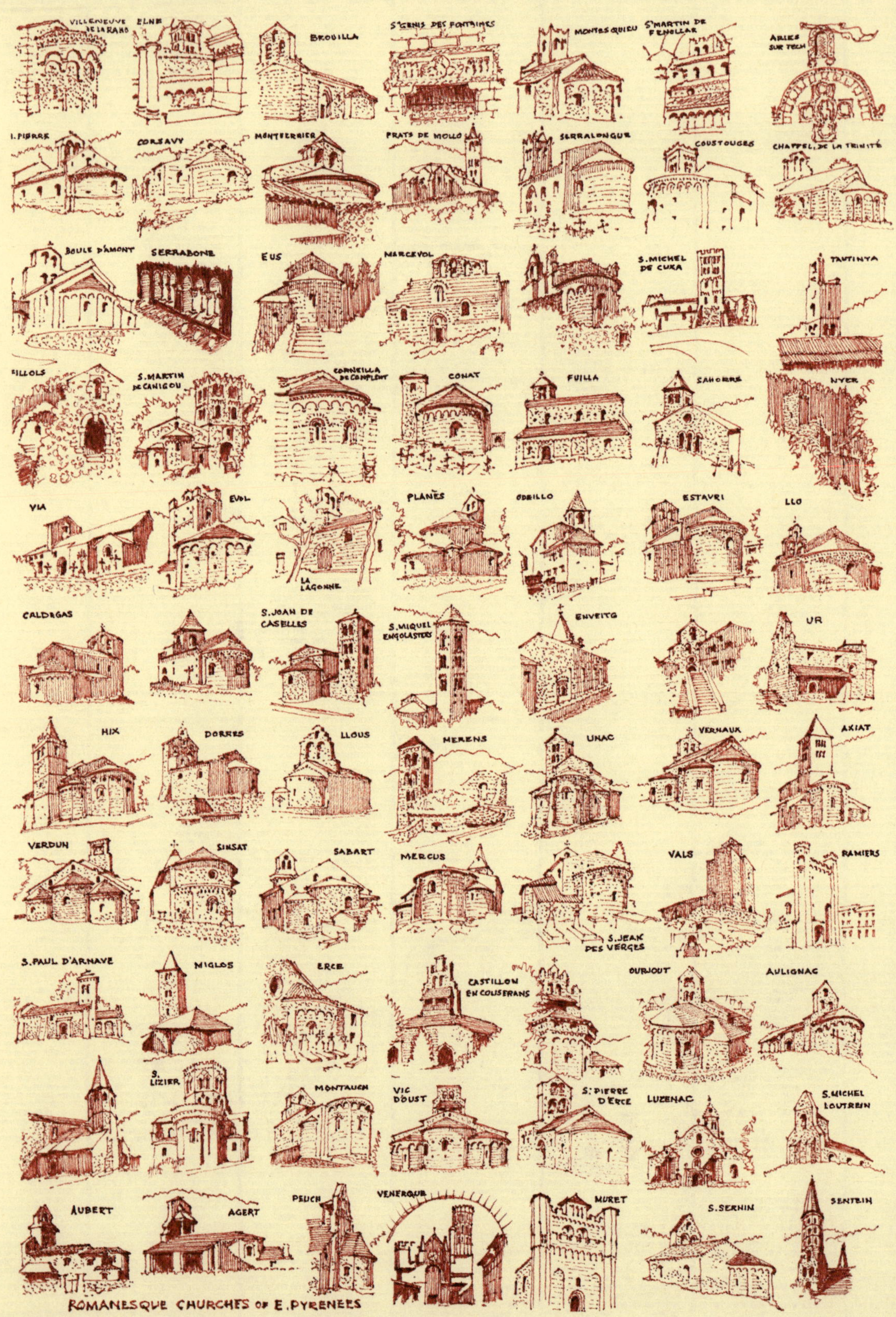

ROMANESQUE CHURCHES OF E.PYRENEES

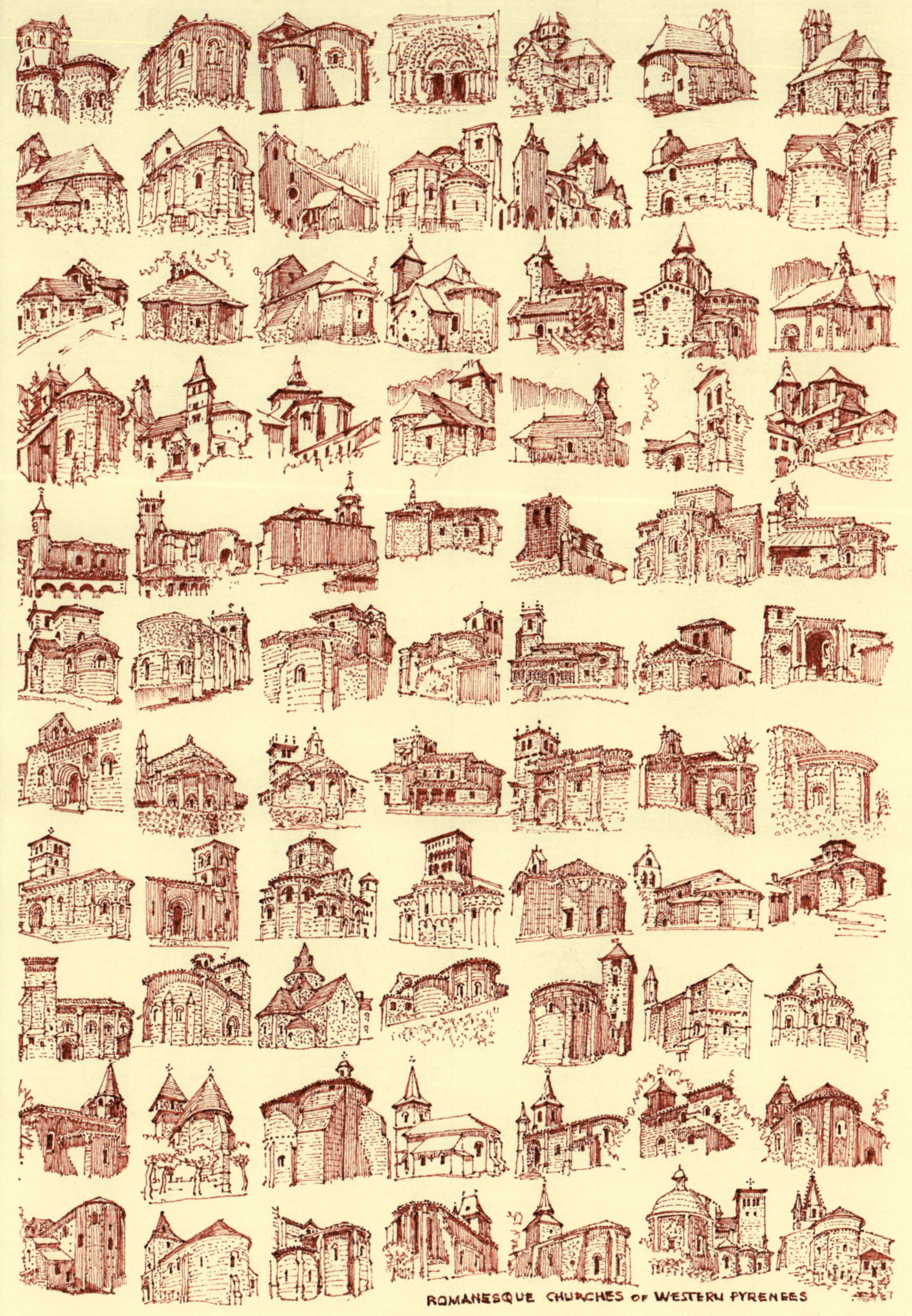
ROMANESQUE CHURCHES OF WESTERN PYRENEES

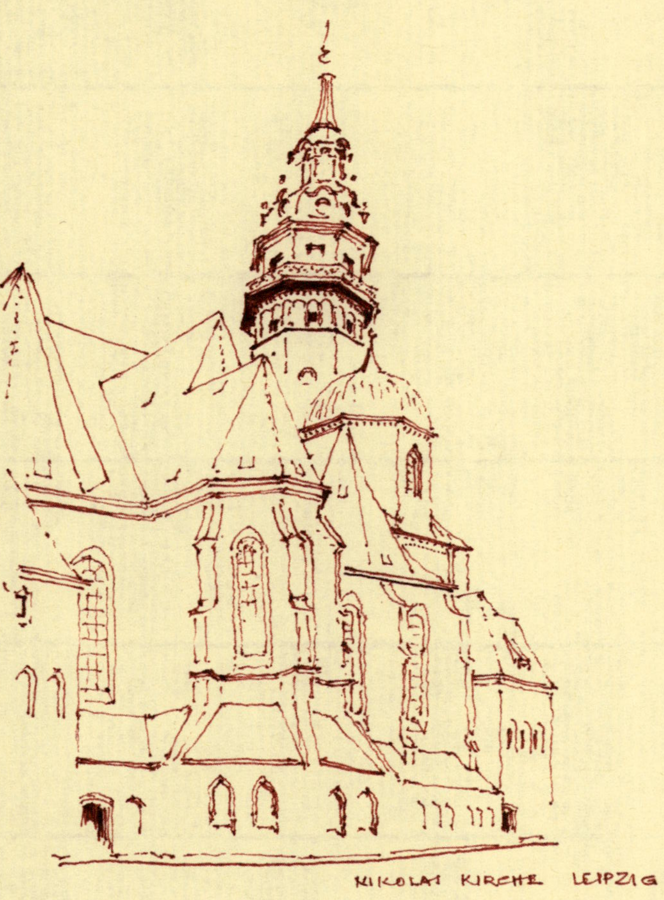
NIKOLAI KIRCHE LEIPZIG

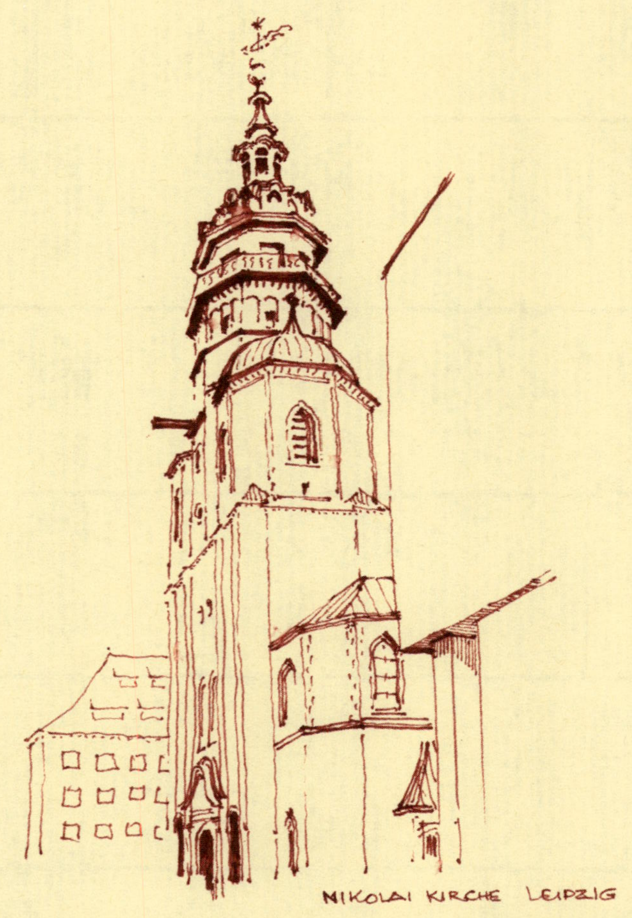
NIKOLAI KIRCHE LEIPZIG

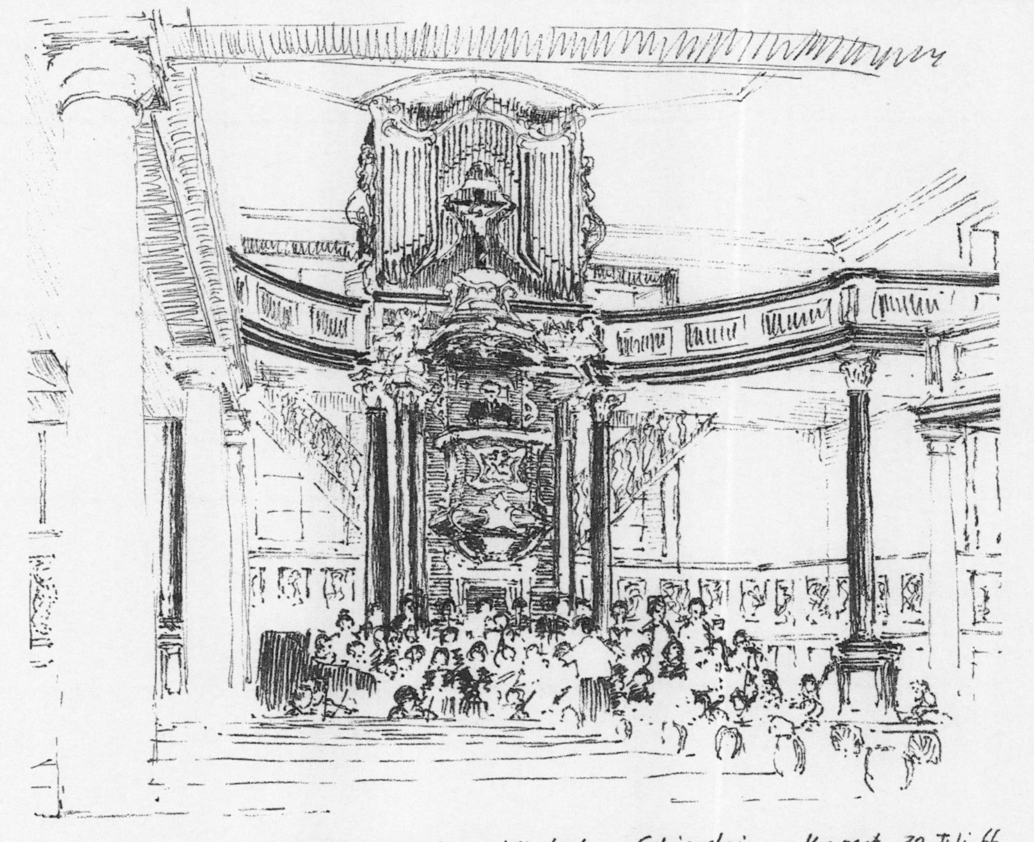

Evangelische Christophoruskirche - Wiesbaden-Schierstein - Konzert 30 Juli 66

The Hemel Hempstead School Orchestra, Creator and Director Lenore Reynel, Leader JAN, Repetiteur Mrs. du Pré.... and so it came to pass that cellist Jacqueline du Pré, with Daniel Barenboim, took a four year lease of the flat in the basement of our house when at the height of her career. Programme: Schubert Mass in D, Britten's St. Nicholas

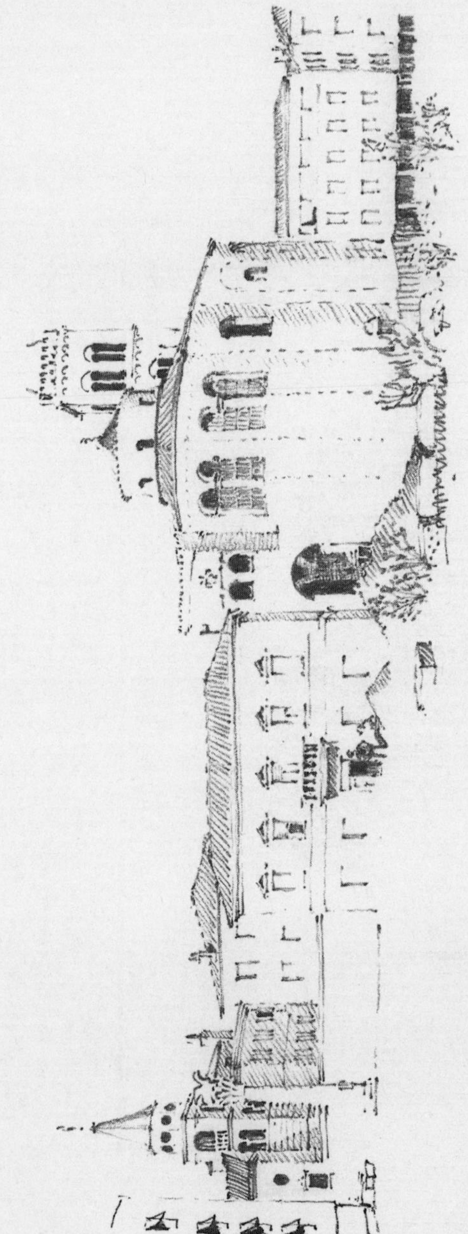

Sv. ILIJA SV DONAT SV STOŠIJA CATHEDRAL

ROMAN FORUM ZADAR

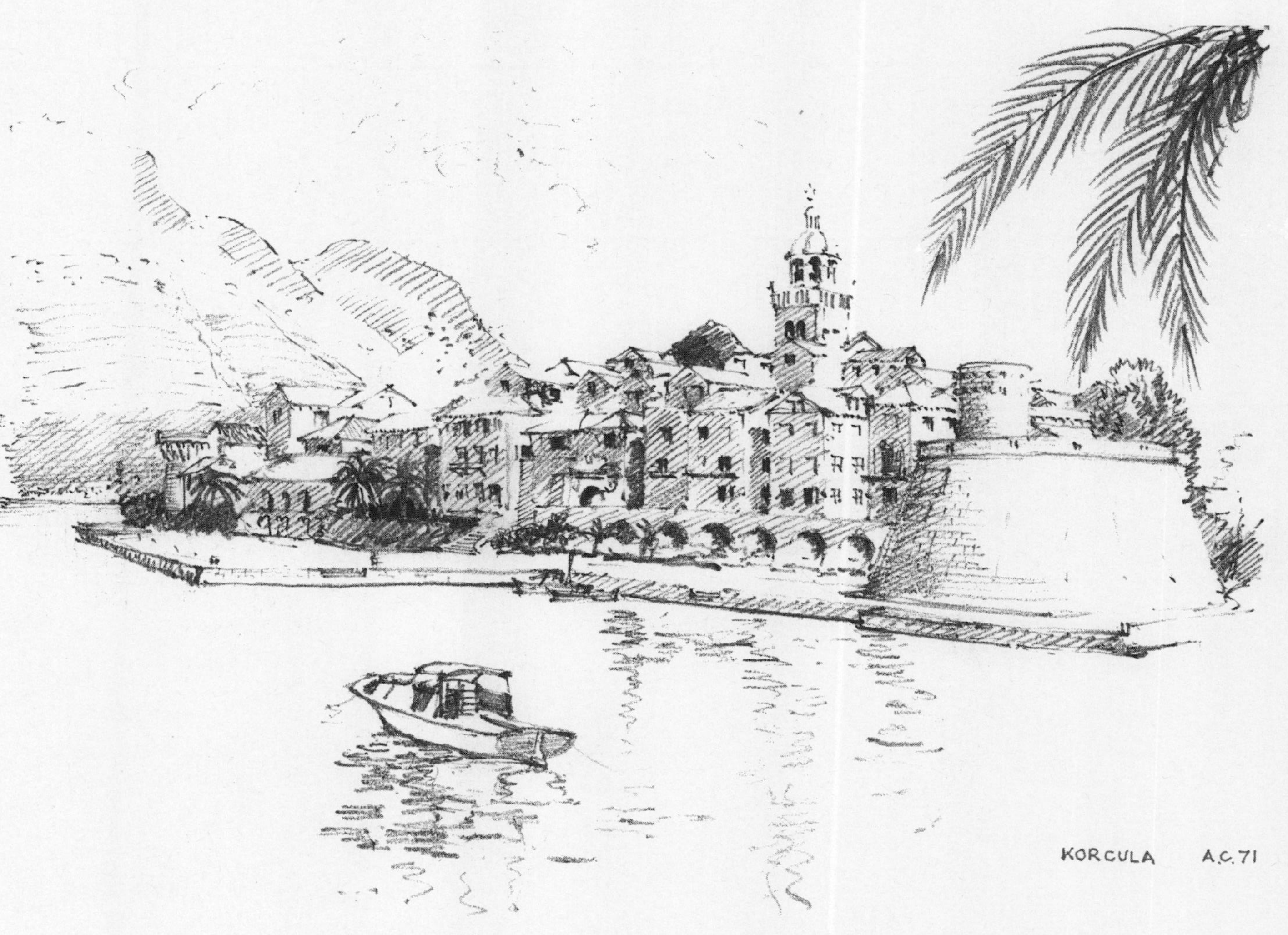
KORCULA A.C.71

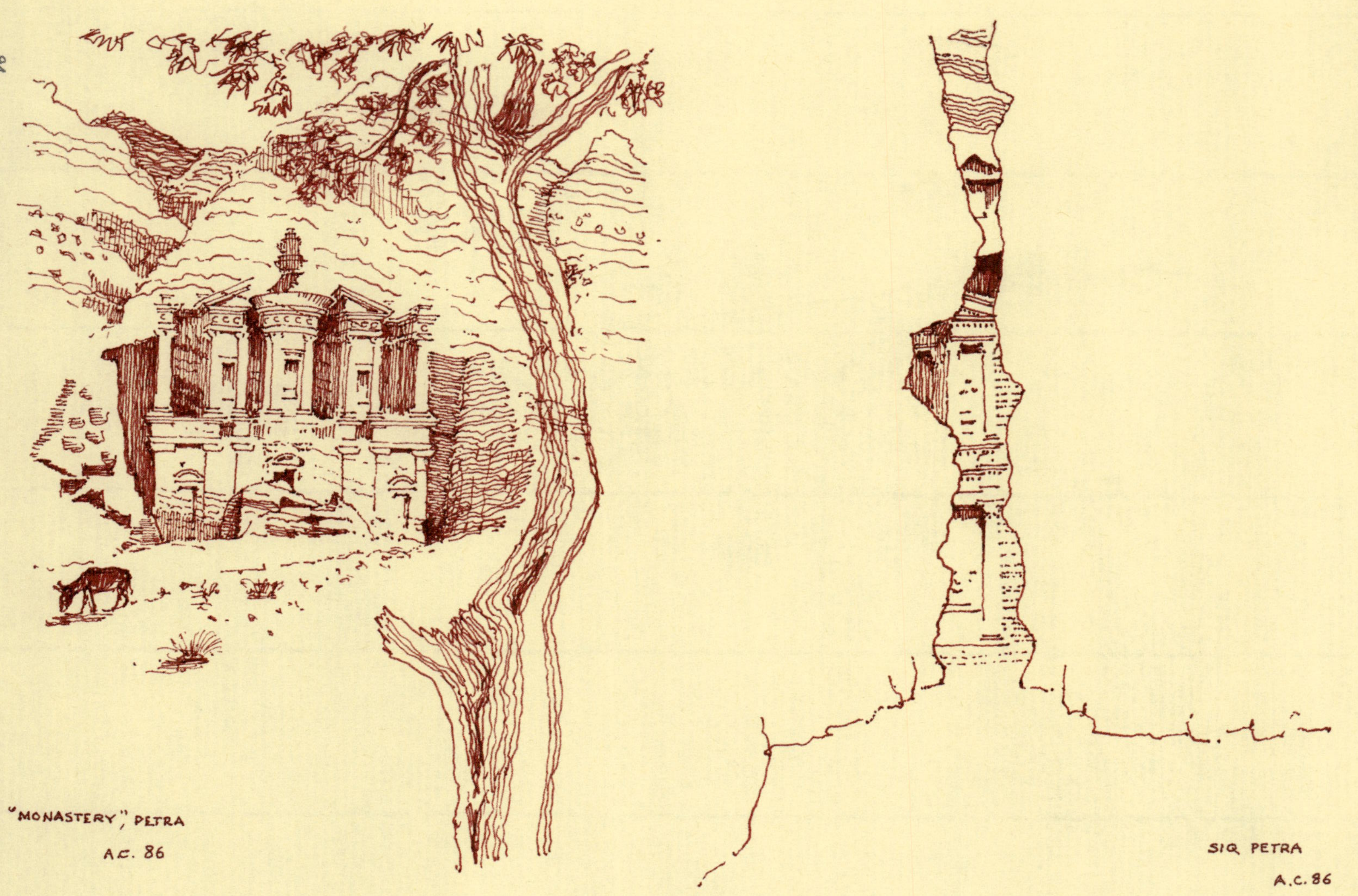
"MONASTERY", PETRA
A.C. 86
SIQ PETRA
A.C. 86

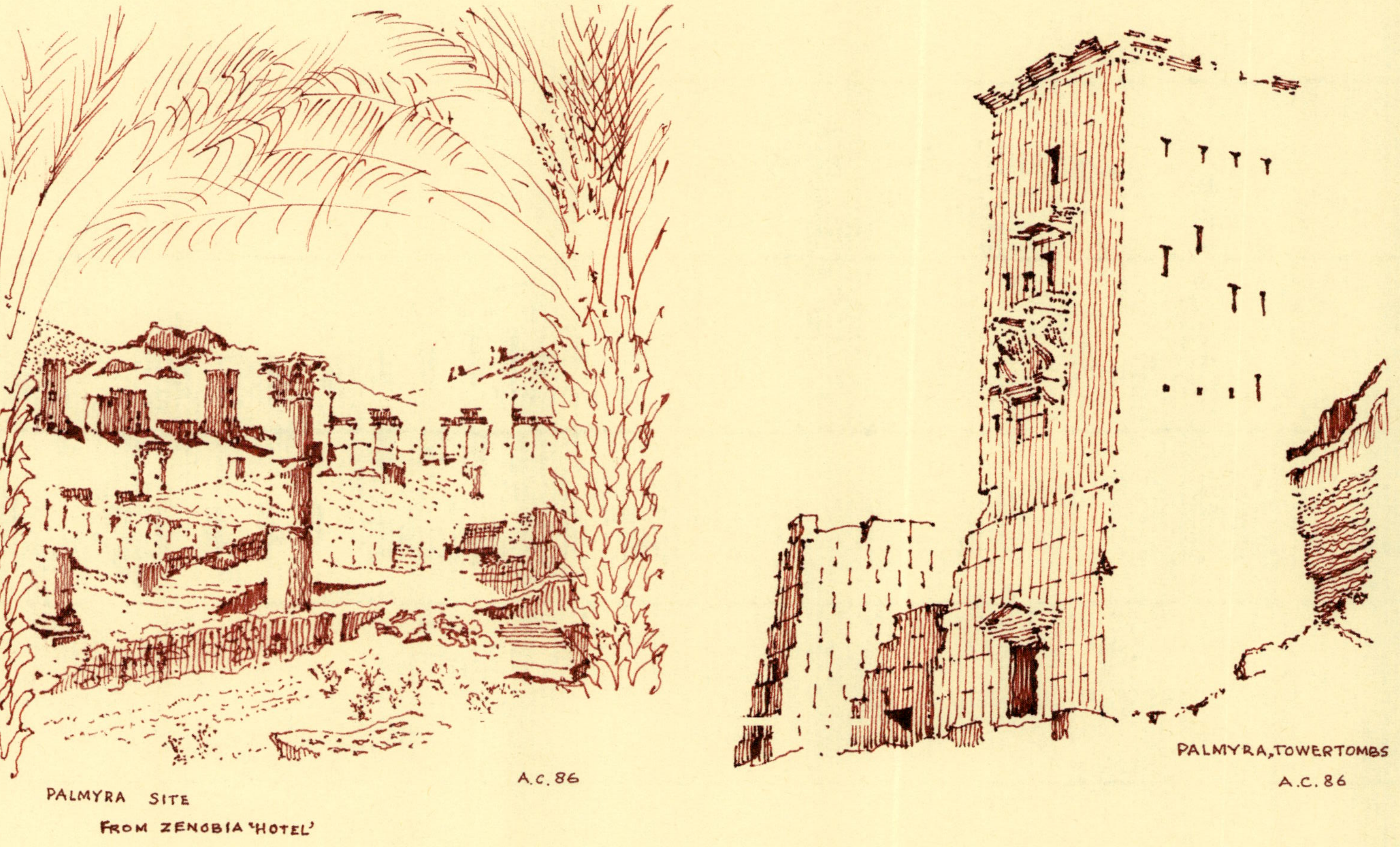
A.C. 86
PALMYRA SITE
FROM ZENOBIA 'HOTEL'
PALMYRA, TOWERTOMBS
A.C. 86

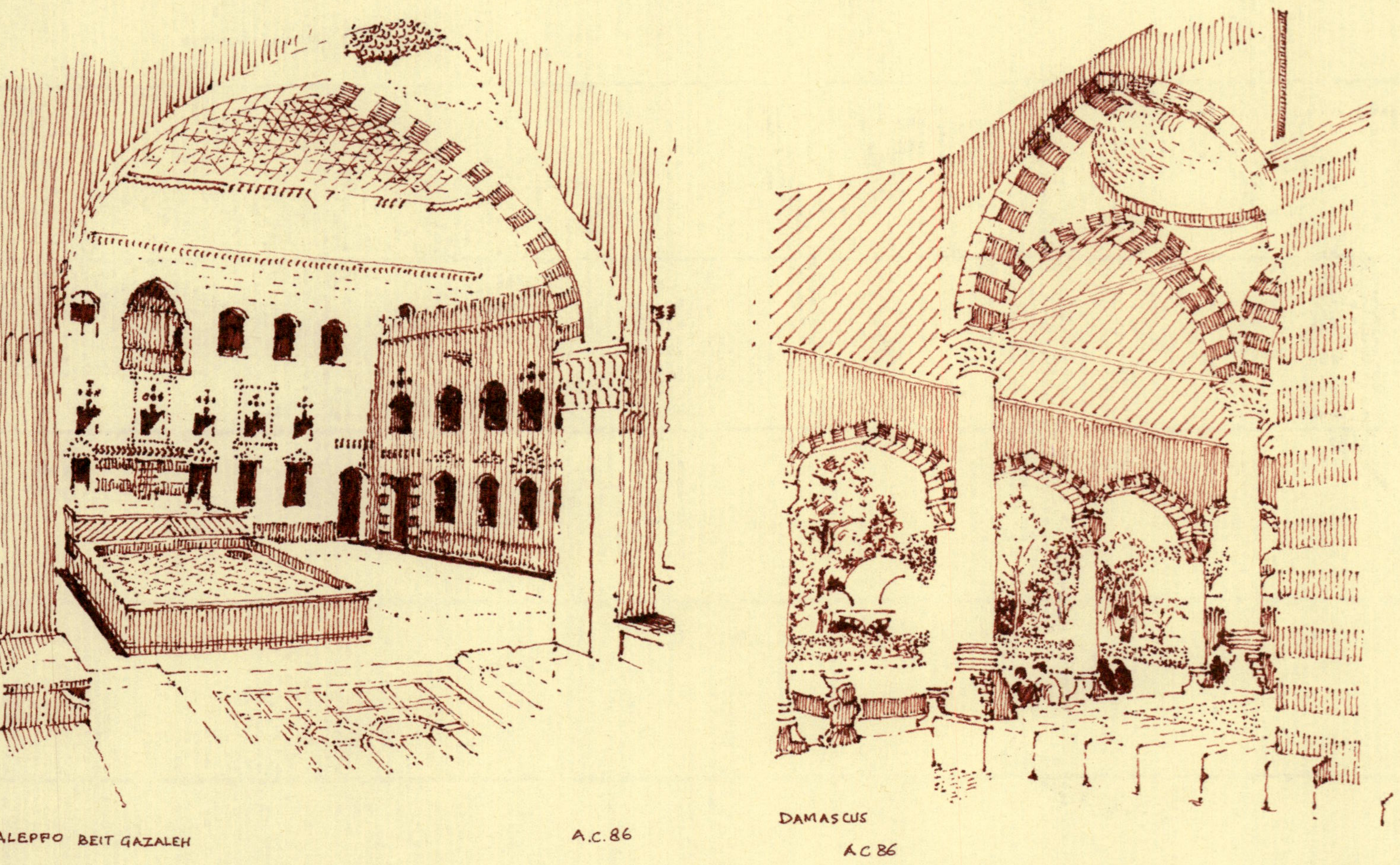
ALEPPO BEIT GAZALEH
A.C.86
DAMASCUS
A.C 86

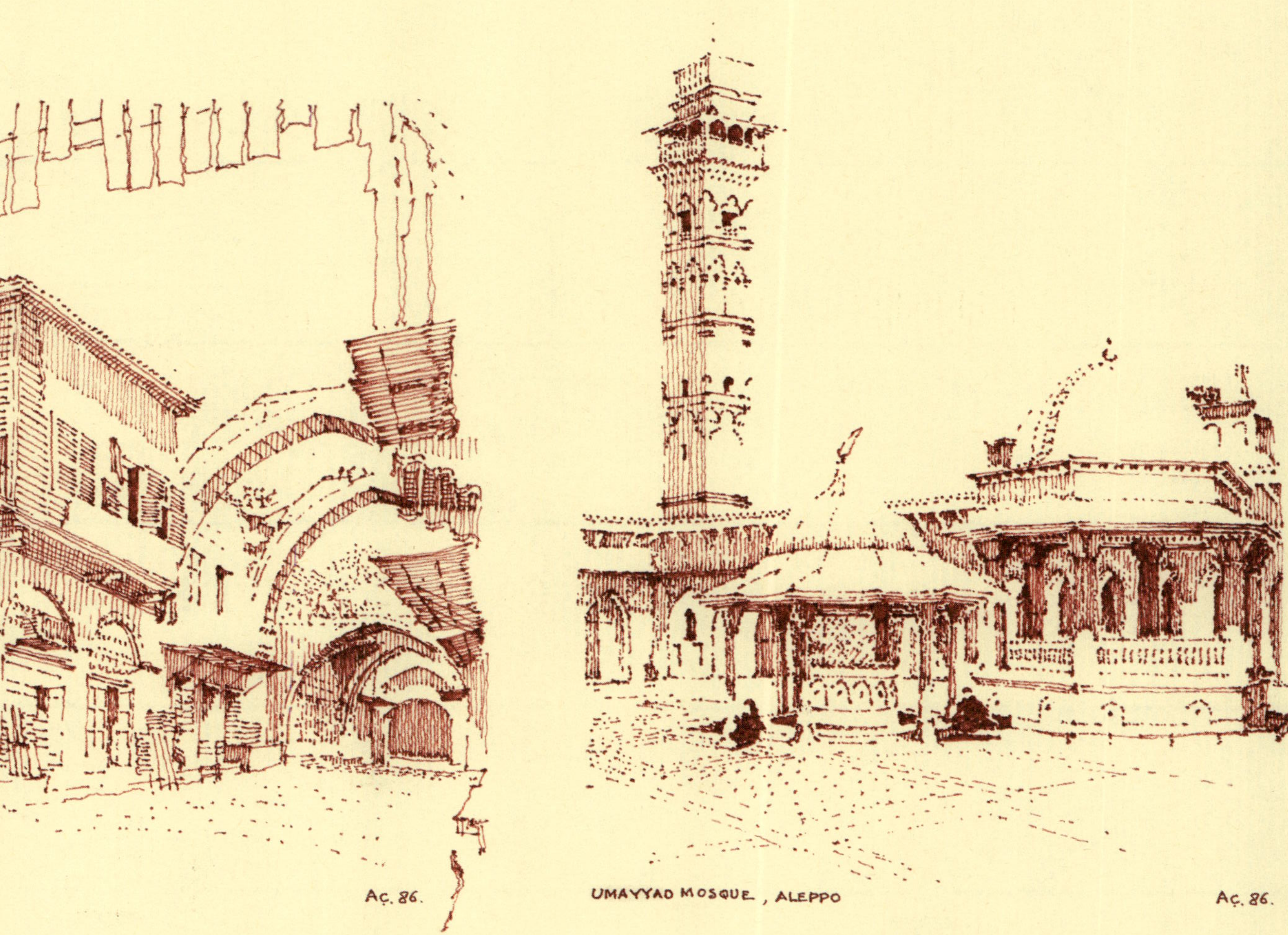

SUQ, ALEPPO

UMAYYAD MOSQUE, ALEPPO

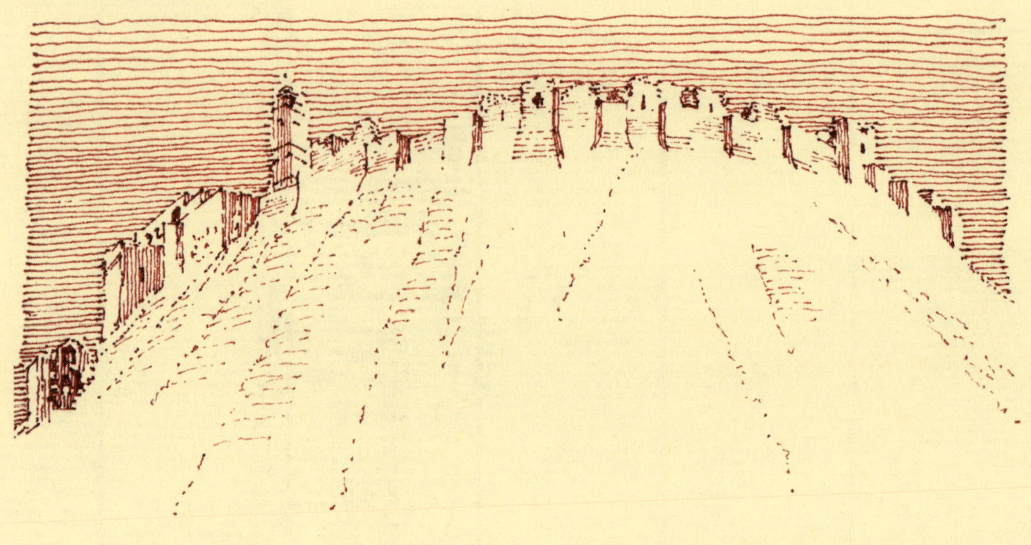

ALEPPO, CITADEL A.C. 86

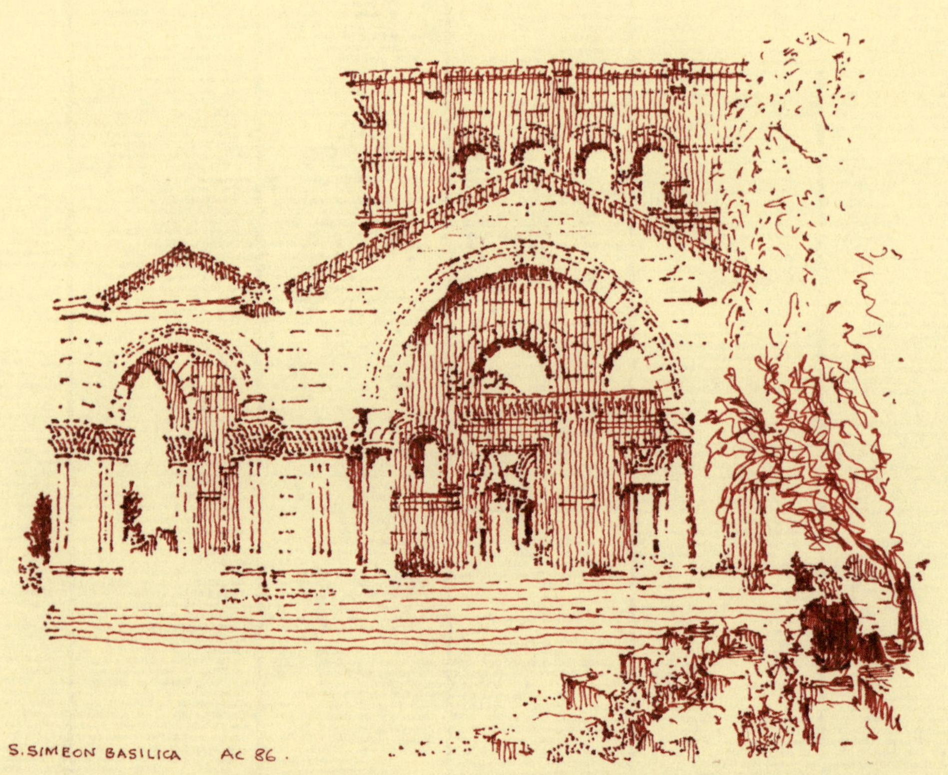

S. SIMEON BASILICA AC 86.

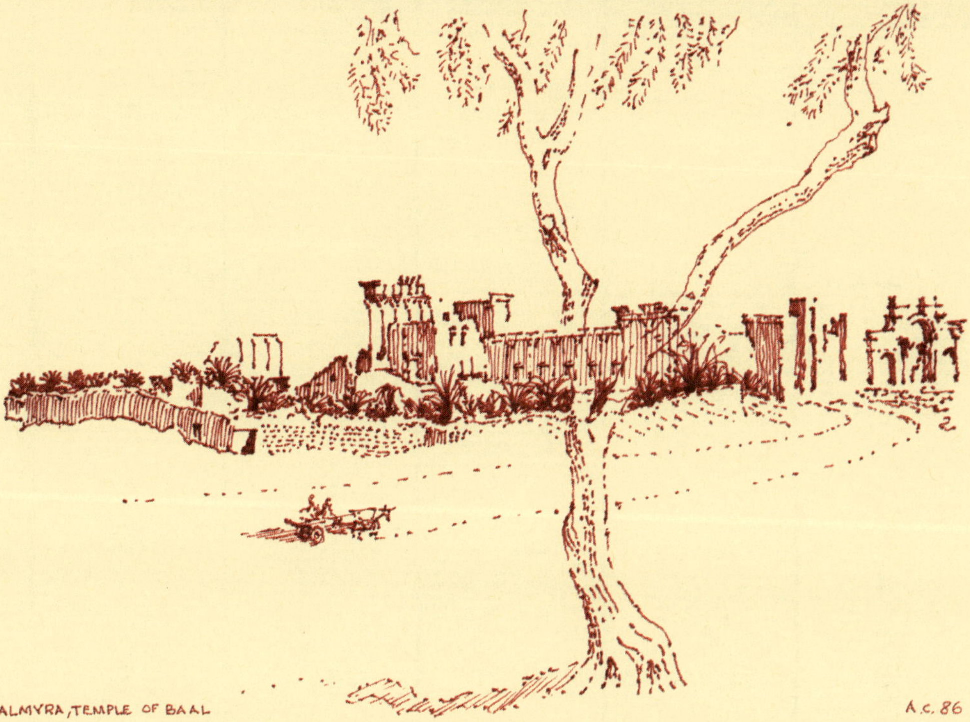

PALMYRA, TEMPLE OF BAAL A.C. 86

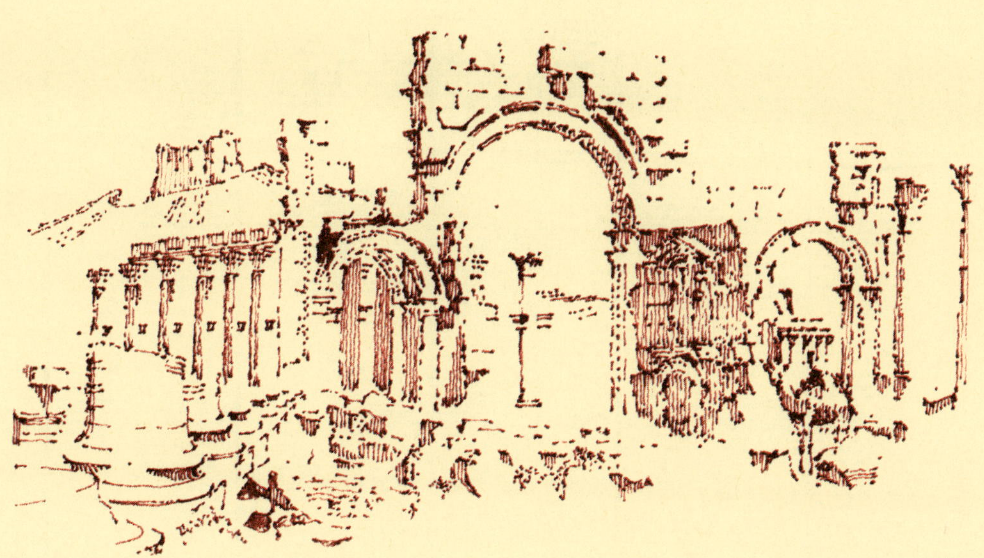

PALMYRA, TRIUMPHAL GATE A.C 86

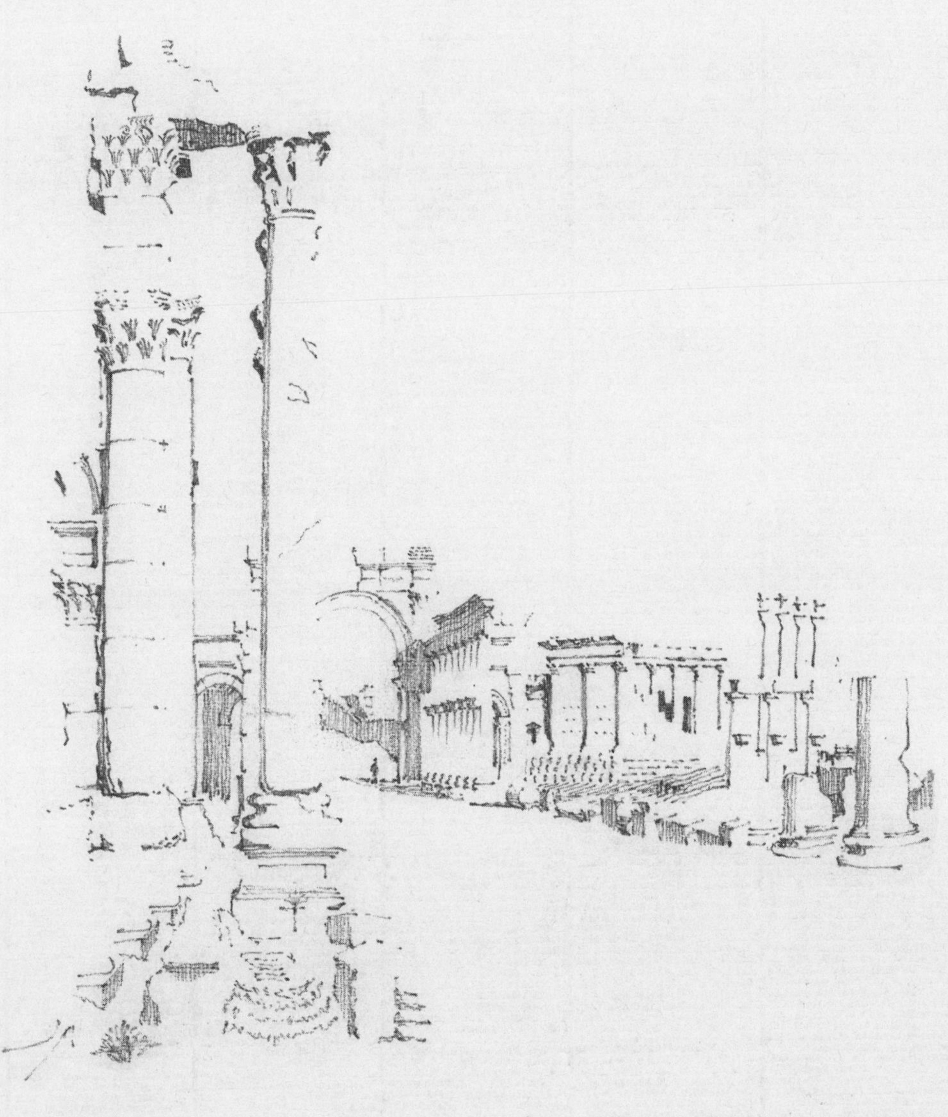

PALMYRA, PROCESSIONAL WAY

AC 86

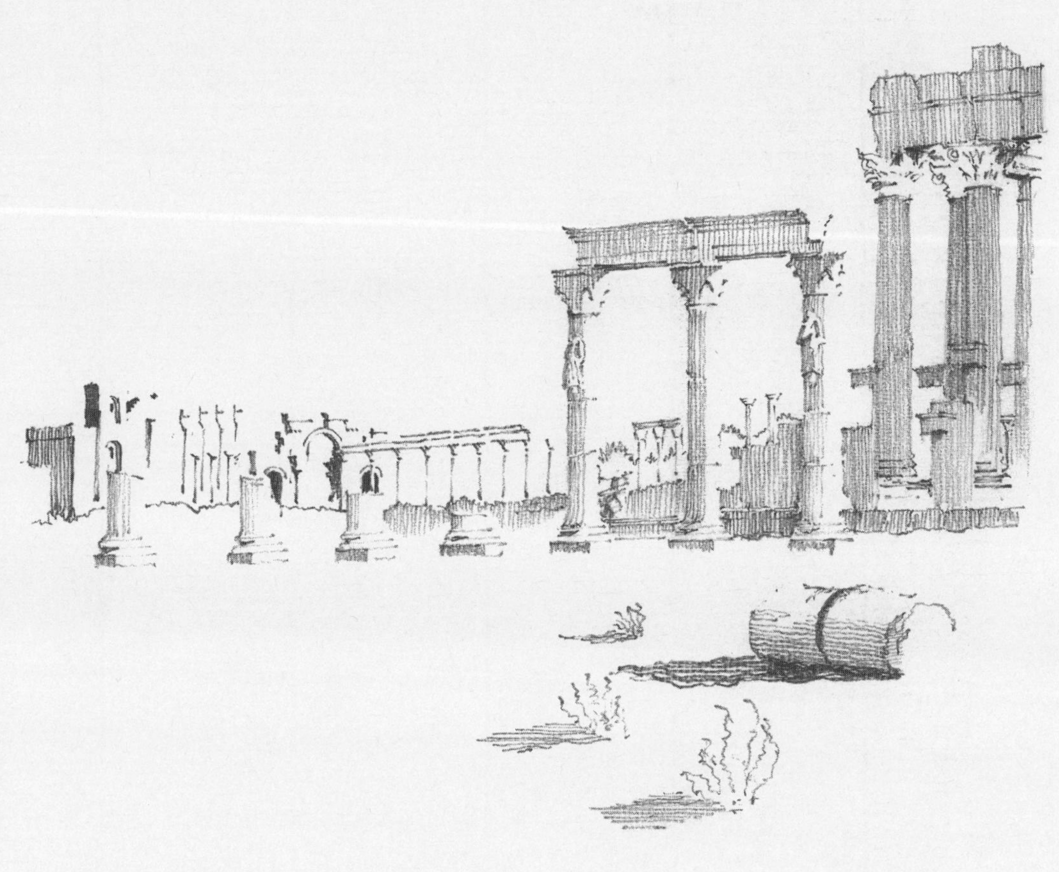

PALMYRA, SITE
AC 86.

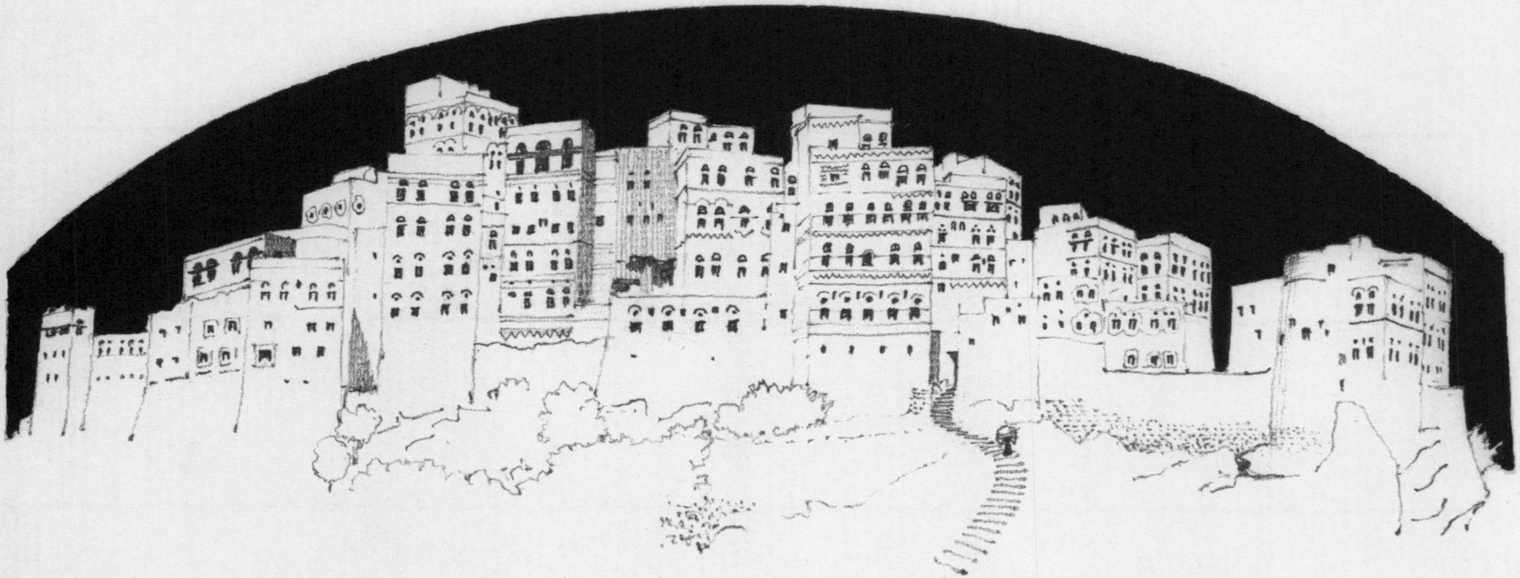

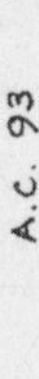

HAJARA A.C. 93

SANAA A.C. 93

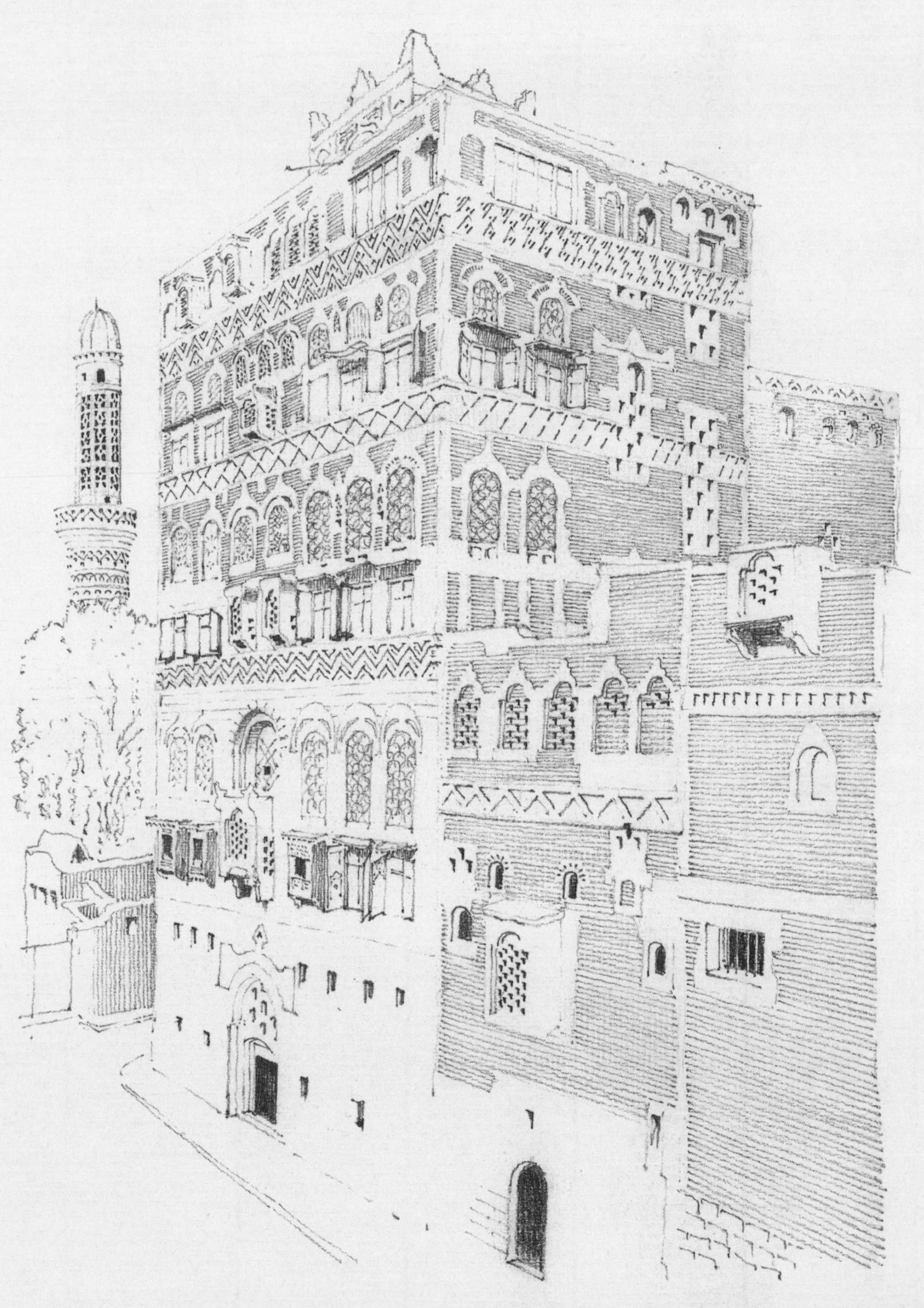

BAYT ZAYID, ALAKWA, SANAA A.C. 93

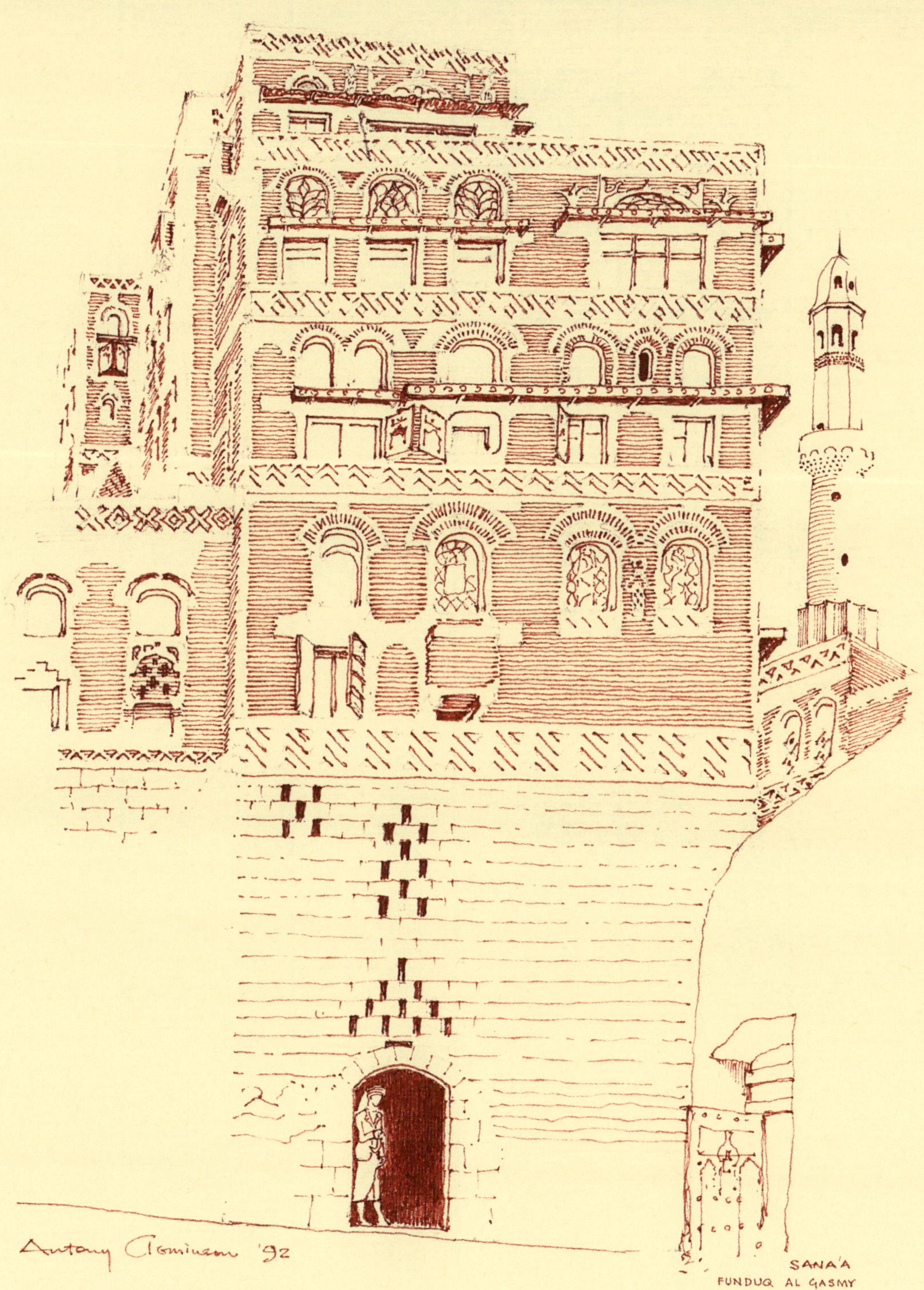
SANA'A
FUNDUQ AL GASMY

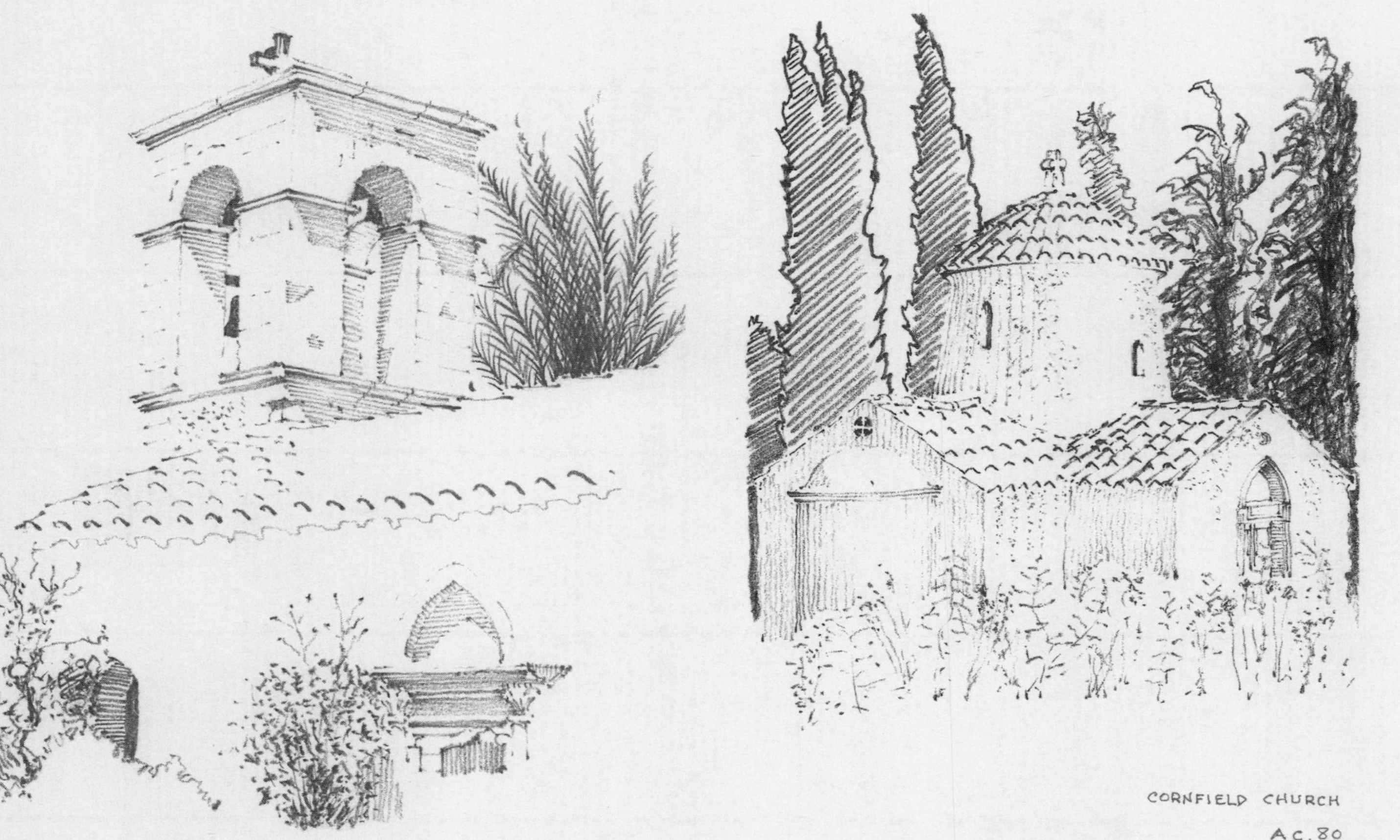
MONI VRONDISIOU A.C. 80

CORNFIELD CHURCH A.C. 80.

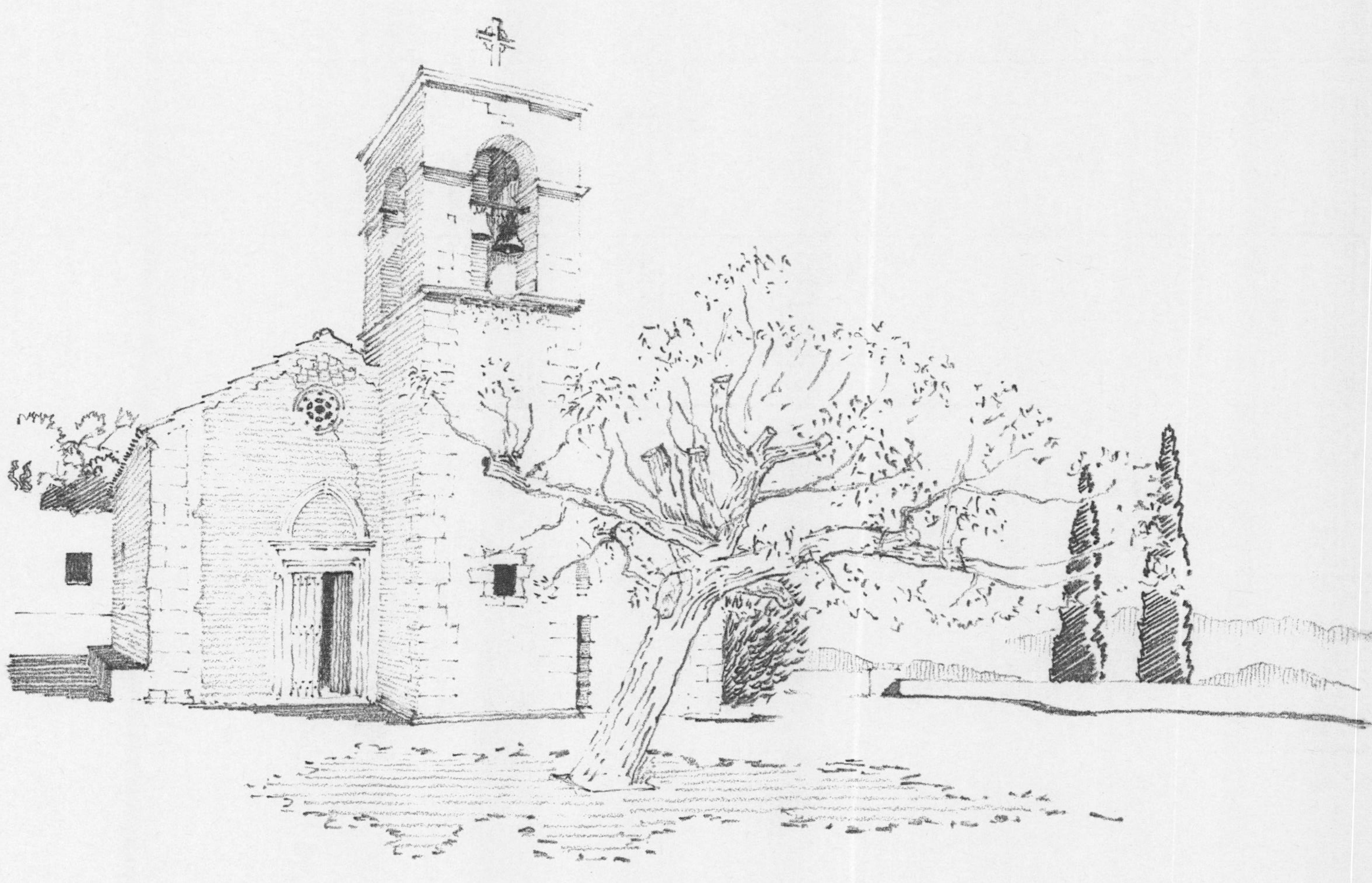

MONI VRONDISIOU A.C. 80

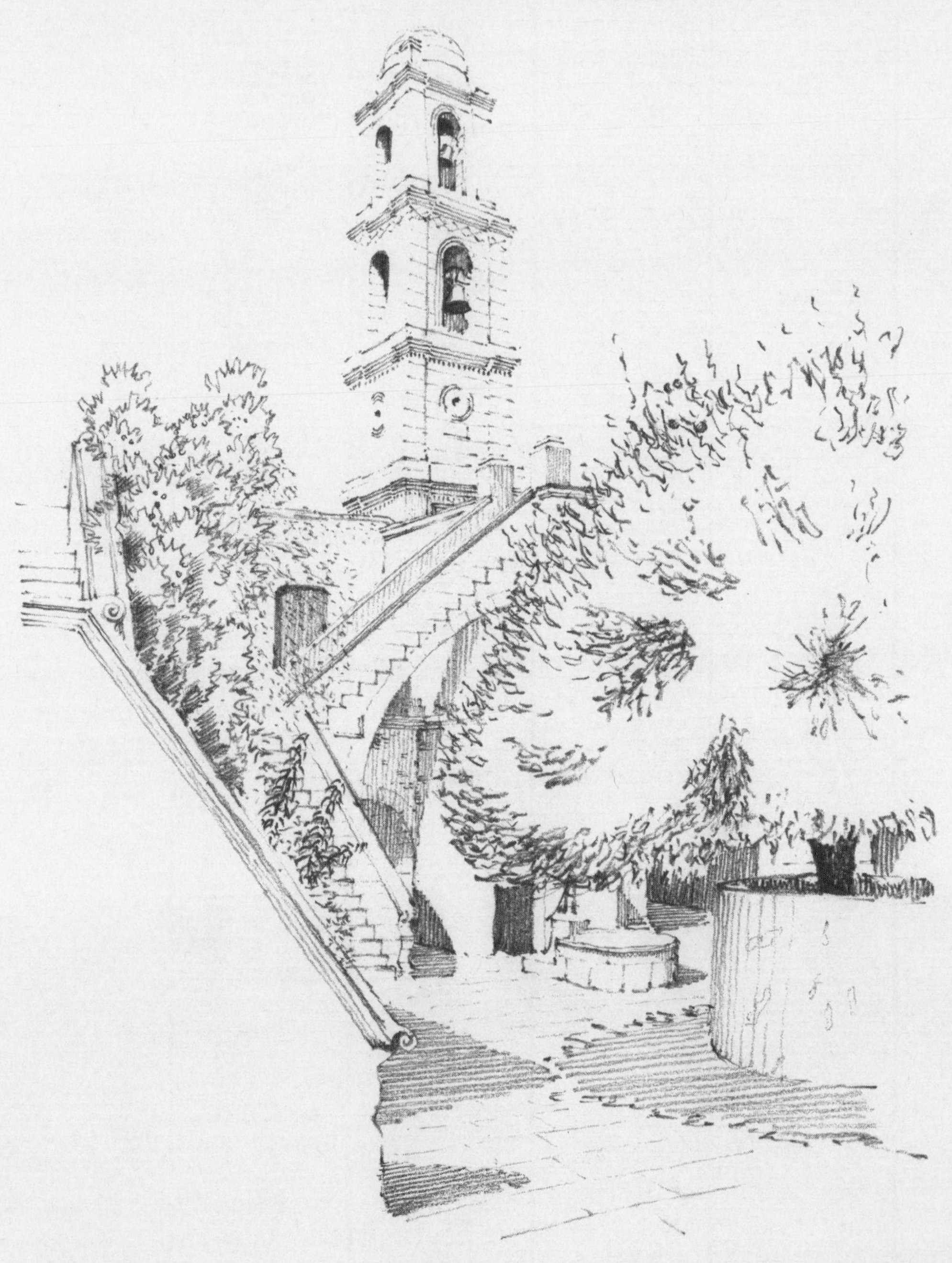

MONI ZAGAROLON AC 80

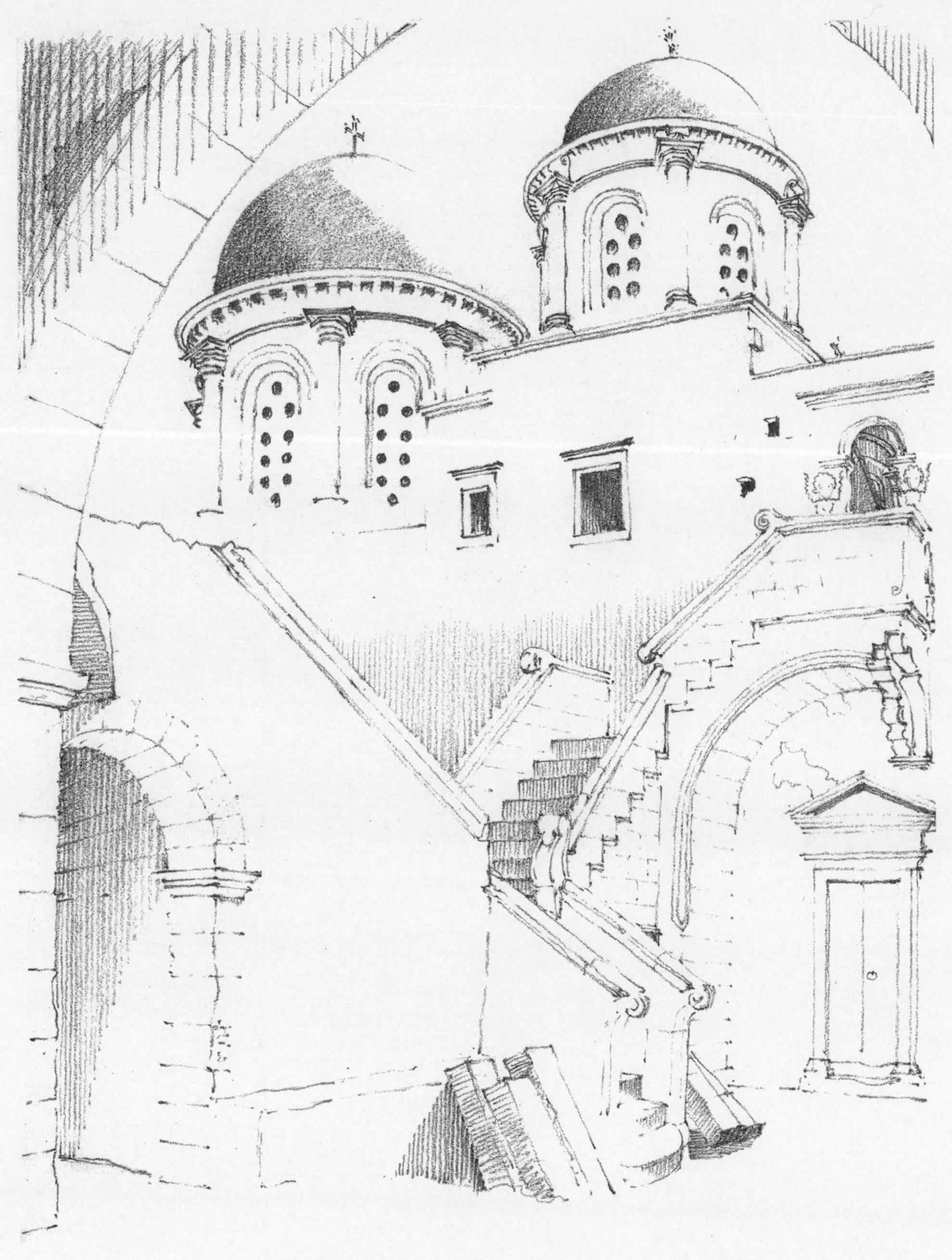

MONI ZAGAROLON AC 80

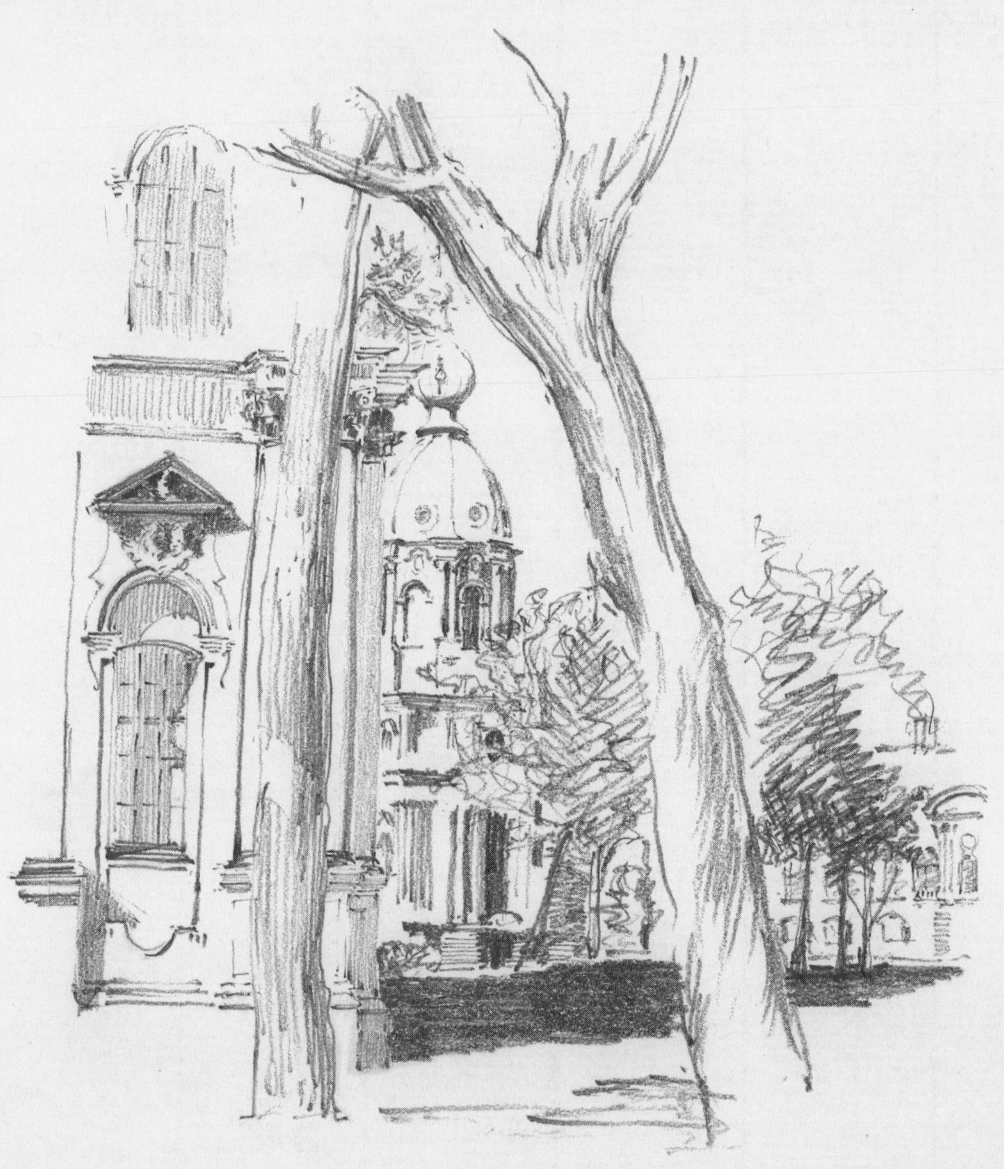

SMOLNY, LENINGRAD   AC 67

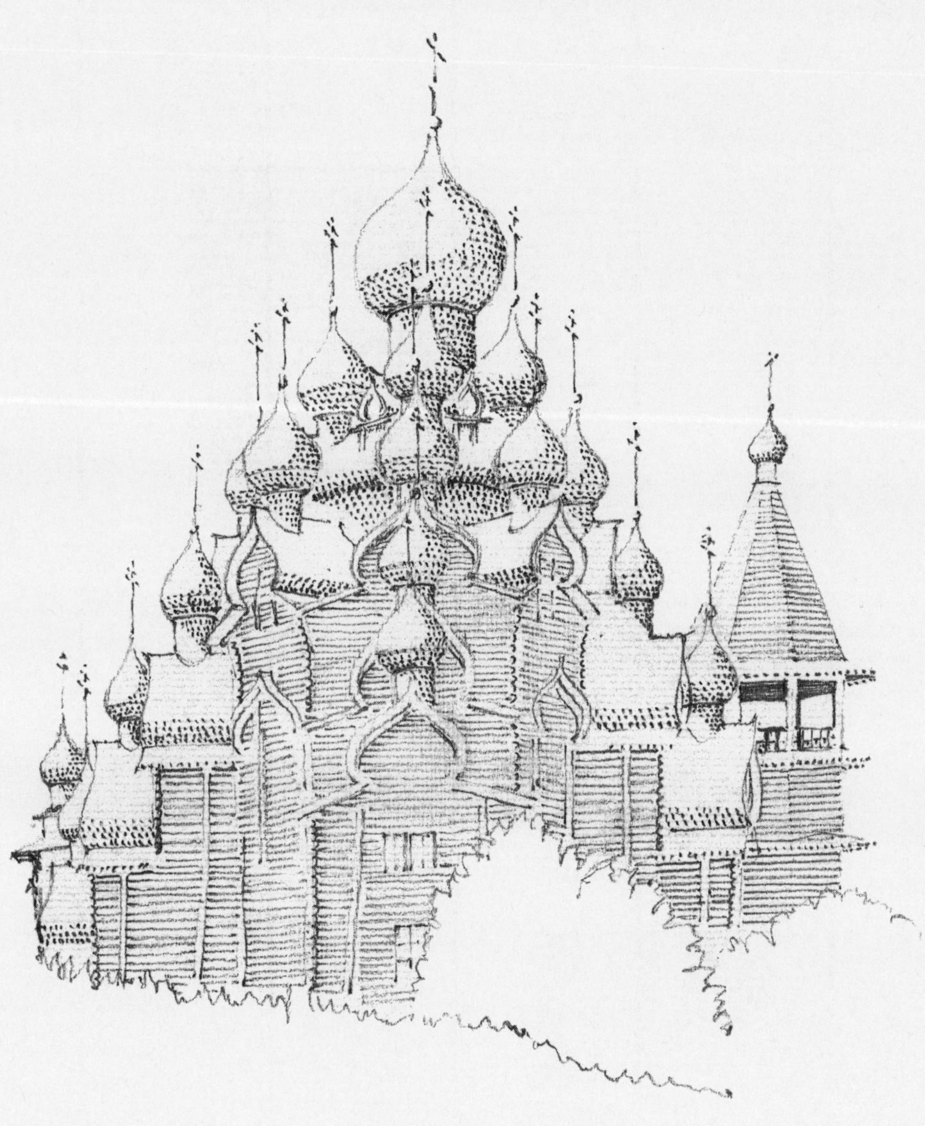

KIZHI, CHURCH OF THE TRANSFIGURATION

A.C. 92

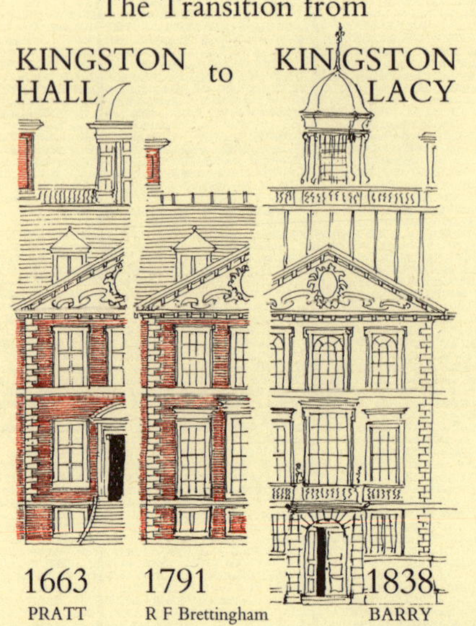

Kingston Hall (since 1838 Kingston Lacy): Architectural Historian for the National Trust, 1982-86; see *Architectural History, Journal of the Society of Architectural Historians of Great Britain*, vol. 31, 1988, pp. 120-135; and *Apollo*, December 1991, pp. 405-409

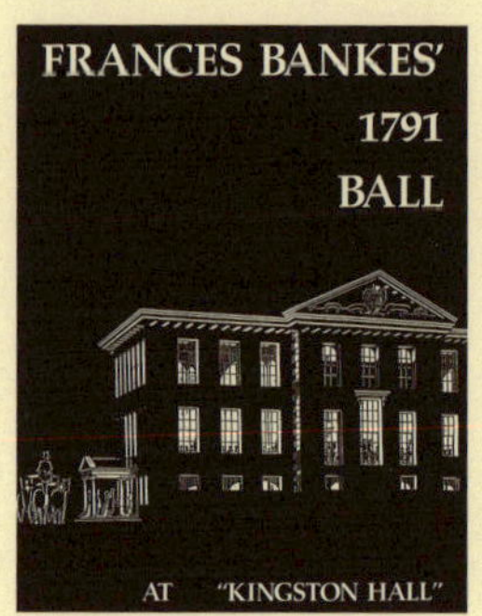

Uppark:
Architectural historian after the fire, 1989-1993 see *Transactions – Journal of the Association for Studies in the Conservation of Historic Buildings*, vol. 15, 1990, pp. 51-55 and vol. 16, 1991, p. 47

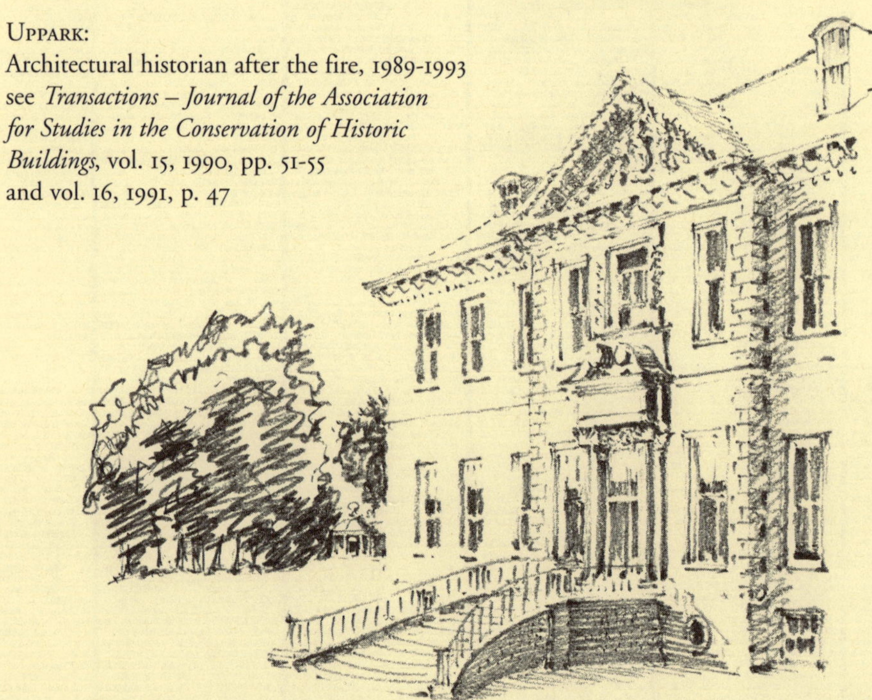

Other studies: *St Helen Bishopsgate*, 1981; *Thomas Archer, his Queen Anne churches and Deptford Parsonage*, 1981; *Thomas Archer's St Philip (Birmingham Cathedral): a case study in stone conservation*, 1982; all available at the Architectural Association library. *Architectural Review* 993, November 1979 – Thirties special edition – 'Silver End beginnings', pp. 302-4